Perspectives on Writing
in Grades 1 - 8

Perspectives on Writing in Grades 1 - 8

Shirley M. Haley-James, Editor
Georgia State University, Atlanta

National Council of Teachers of English
1111 Kenyon Road, Urbana, Illinois 61801

NCTE Editorial Board: Paul T. Bryant, Marilyn Hanf Buckley, Thomas J. Creswell, C. Kermeen Fristrom, Jane M. Hornburger, Robert F. Hogan, *ex officio*, Paul O'Dea, *ex officio*

Staff Editor: Barbara Davis

Book Design: Tom Kovacs

NCTE Stock Number: 35196

Library of Congress Cataloging in Publication Data

Main entry under title:

Perspectives on writing in grades 1–8.

An activity of the NCTE Committee on Teaching Written Composition in Elementary Schools.
Bibliography: p.
1. English language—Composition and exercises.
I. Haley-James, Shirley M.   II. National Council of Teachers of English. Committee on Teaching Written Composition in Elementary Schools.
LB1631.P43   372.6'23   81-3994
ISBN 0-8141-3519-6   AACR2

Contents

Acknowledgments vii

Introduction ix

1. Twentieth-Century Perspectives on Writing in Grades
One through Eight 3
   Shirley M. Haley-James

2. Classroom Teachers' Reports on Teaching Written
Composition 19
   Walter T. Petty
   Patrick J. Finn

3. A "Whole-Language Approach" Writing Program 35
   Vera Milz

4. A Functional Writing Program for the Middle Grades 43
   Joanne Yatvin

5. Romance Precedes Precision: Recommended Classroom
Teaching Practices 59
   Marlene Caroselli

6. A District-Wide Plan for the Evaluation of Student
Writing 73
   Roger McCaig

7. A New Look at Research on Writing 93
   Donald Graves

8. Writing in Grades One through Eight: Summary
Reflections 117
   Shirley M. Haley-James

References 121

Acknowledgments

Formed in 1976, the National Council of Teachers of English Committee on Teaching Written Composition in Elementary Schools has reviewed and interpreted authoritative opinion and research literature related to teaching written composition in the elementary school and called attention to composition programs and teaching practices that deserved further emphasis. This monograph reports the findings of the committee.

Some individual committee members authored chapters of this monograph; other members helped create and shape what became the final manuscript by serving as advisors and as chapter reviewers. Ruth Carlson, one of the committee members scheduled to author a chapter, died before she was able to pursue the assignment. The committee would like to acknowledge her contributions not only to NCTE but also to the profession of English language arts education.

Although the primary audience of this work is the classroom teacher in grades one through eight, the monograph relates to an area of particular interest also to supervisors, curriculum coordinators, school administrators, and teacher-educators.

Introduction

History has taught us that writing is important to the individual during each stage of life. Learning to help children gain confidence and experience in writing is an important part of the classroom teacher's role. Even for the very young, writing is a means of thinking, learning, and being. Carefully stimulated and supported writing experiences enhance any child's development.

The historical review of authoritative opinion regarding appropriate instruction in written composition in grades one through eight, presented in Chapter 1, addresses five basic questions. The recommendations of those authorities cited are distilled into eleven observations about effective writing instruction. These observations, in turn, provide a philosophical framework for all that follows.

Chapter 2 cites the data gleaned by Walter T. Petty and Patrick J. Finn in their random survey of teaching practices in use in fourth-grade classrooms. The results of the survey, and Petty and Finn's interpretation of those results, suggest that while some of the teaching practices utilized are in concert with those recommended by the authorities cited in Chapter 1, other practices are in direct conflict with a substantial body of professional literature. Contrasting specific recommendations made in Chapter 1 with teaching practices reported in Chapter 2 poses significant questions not only for teachers but also for teacher-educators.

Reports of other successful current classroom teaching practices and writing programs are detailed in Chapters 3 through 6. These chapters discuss the importance of a specific purpose and audience for a piece of writing as well as the necessity for prewriting, rewriting, and evaluating writing. All writing programs, teaching practices, and evaluation procedures in this collection illustrate the recommendations of widely recognized authorities.

Chapter 7 details the trends of writing-related research in the past fifty years, the role of the classroom teacher in such research, more recent developments in research practices, and the future research needs of students, teachers, and policy-makers. Specific research questions in areas of teacher and writer development and the development of a new means of assessing the quality of student writing are posed, emphasizing the necessity of conducting writing research in context.

Concluding with an overall summary, these eight chapters have one over-arching purpose: to help teachers help children in grades one through eight gain experience, confidence, and skill in writing.

Shirley M. Haley-James
January 1981

Perspectives on Writing in Grades 1 – 8

Twentieth-Century Perspectives on Writing in Grades One through Eight

Shirley M. Haley-James
Georgia State University, Atlanta

Suzanne Prince replaced the cap on the end of her felt tip marker. The class story about the interview with Officer Huggins was charted and ready for her students to read when they returned in the morning. She hung the four sheets of chart paper along the rim of the board and moved her students' individually written stories about Officer Huggins' visit over to the book-binding table. Glancing at the story on the top of the stack, she recalled the excitement about writing and reading that the interviewing program she had initiated just a few weeks before had generated in her first graders.

Before beginning the program, Suzanne had not thought it possible that first graders could learn to select and invite their own special classroom guests, conduct successful interviews, write individual and group stories based upon interview sessions, and read those stories to the class. However, with some help from the local language arts supervisor, Suzanne established a program that was rich in oral language and listening; one that generated student writing that was actually meant to be read.

Adding the interviewing program to her already established curriculum, Suzanne related her own valid teaching practices to the teaching practices other professionals had learned were also important in the teaching of writing: She made personal "connections" that improved her instruction.

There are countless teachers at every level who know what works for them, but seek also to learn what others have found productive. They want to help their students improve their writing, to relate other successful teaching practices to their students' needs. Out of the research on writing they want to extract procedures that have stood the test of time and new techniques backed by a strong theoretical base. They want to place the demands to improve their students' writing in the context of this body of professional knowledge.

This presentation of authoritative opinion concerning the teaching of writing in grades one through eight is prepared with such teachers in mind. As background for its preparation, professional literature published in the United States between 1900 and 1980 was studied and summarized. This process generated numerous subtopics, all of which centered around five questions about children and their writing:

1. Why should elementary school age children write?
2. When should elementary age children write?
3. What should elementary age children write about?
4. How can teachers best help elementary school age children with their writing?
5. How can teachers best evaluate the writing of elementary school age children?

These five questions provide the basic structure for this review of professional literature related to writing and writing instruction.

Prior to researching the literature, criteria for selecting material to review were established—that an author's work had been published repeatedly in national education journals or books and cited by others in the field, and that the author was generally regarded as an authority on instruction in writing. Applying these criteria to literature published from 1900 through 1980 produced such a volume of material that it would be unwieldy to cite all of it in this chapter. Thus, a selection of related literature will be presented; additional citations will be included in the list of references.

Why Should Elementary School Age Children Write?

A hundred people chosen at random would probably say first (and perhaps exclusively) that children need to learn to write so that they will be able to convey personal messages and other information to those not present who would not otherwise receive those messages or that information. That is, writing is seen as pragmatic in function.

Various authorities, such as Paul Witty (1941), Donald Murray (1973), and Harry Greene and Walter Petty (1975), have discussed this pragmatic advantage of writing. Indeed, that writing is practical and important seems axiomatic, and the professional literature reflects that authorities share this perception. By no means, however, is the communication of personal messages and other information perceived to be the only advantage of writing. Since the late 1930s, a great deal has also been written about the psychological and personal learning values of writing.

Writing's psychological value to children has been documented by so many since 1939 that citing even the major authorities who have discussed it would be impractical. Committees and commissions of NCTE and numerous individual authorities have stressed the tension release and escape value of getting feelings on paper and of reflecting through writing on troublesome, victorious, or otherwise important personal experiences. Being able through writing to think about nameless things, explore fears, and synthesize all types of experiences are other psychological values of writing that these authors have proposed. Alvina Treut Burrows (1951, 1952) also points out that through writing, children maintain individuality and independence in an adult-dominated world and maintain their powers of invention in the face of an onslaught of mass media entertainment.

Personal learning values of writing stem from discovery. Through seeing personal ideas and experiences appear on paper, redrafting what is written to make it more accurate or complete, and receiving reader feedback on what has been written, a writer expands what is learned from the original experience. Being involved in, and yet in a sense detached from, experiences that have been recorded on paper encourages insight and discovery.

The expansion of learning that writing encourages is less likely to develop through strictly oral communication because of the transient nature of oral language.

Burrows (1952 and 1972) stressed personal learning values of writing. Her emphasis on personal learning through writing has been reinforced by authorities such as Janet Emig (1977), Donald Graves (1978), and the NCTE Committee on Writing Standards (1979).

Though the effects of writing experiences on a student's reading comprehension have been mentioned only occasionally in the past, more research on this subject is currently underway. In the mid and late seventies, writing was credited by authorities such as David Elkind (1976) and Donald Graves (1978) with enhancing reading comprehension. Elkind noted that reading and writing are reciprocal processes. Children learning how to structure ideas in writing also learn to recognize ways in which reading material may be structured. Graves points out that children who write for others achieve more easily the objectivity necessary for reading the work of others.

When Should Elementary School Age Children Write?

When children should write can be discussed from several perspectives; one such perspective concerns at what age children can learn to write. There is a school of thought that distinguishes handwriting from writing that is meaning-based for the child, and proposes that young school age children must learn to form all of the letters before learning to write meaningful material. Thus, written composition is delayed until second or even third grade. This idea is represented only marginally in the professional literature, but published teaching materials frequently appear to have been developed from such a perspective.

Recent authoritative opinion runs directly counter to this position. James Moffett (1979) emphasizes that, even in the initial stages of learning, lettering needs to be connected to meaning, to symbolizing the child's inner speech as related to personal perceptions and experiences. Donald Graves (1979) reports that we underestimate what children can and should do the first day and week of their schooling. Whereas Graves used to think that children needed to be able to read in order to write, his observations have recently led him to conclude that children who know how to form as few as six consonants and the sounds that those consonants represent can begin writing, and their writing can be decoded. In context, "fiv" can be understood as "five" and "gob" can be understood as "job." Shirley Haley-James and David Hobson (1980) have described an effective meaning-based oral language, writing, and reading instructional approach.

Just as when children should write is important, how frequently they write is important. In this matter, authoritative opinion is remarkably consistent. Mildred Dawson (1956), Eileen Tway (1975), Charles Cooper (1976), and Philip Lopate (1978) are representative of the many authorities who urge teachers to encourage children to write frequently and establish an atmosphere in which children expect to engage in purposeful writing at various times of the day. In 1975, the NCTE Commission on Composition summarized the views of these and other authorities: Children learn to write by writing; they need to write quite frequently.

While assessing writing programs across the United States, Graves (1978) observed that the most severe problem in elementary school writing programs was *no* writing. Too much attention was being paid in schools to writing as an etiquette-bound event, and not enough to writing as a means of personal communication. Graves's observation addresses both the importance of frequent writing and another aspect of when children should write: They should write when they sense a need or a desire to write.

Prominent authorities from the 1920s through the 1970s have emphasized the importance of a student's personal desire to write. Howard Driggs (1923) stressed that students should write when they feel *impelled*, not *compelled* by someone else, to express themselves. Hughes Mearns (1926) referred to this as the writing "idea," the vague but insistent feeling of a need to compose. Harry A. Greene (1937) related the need to compose to a particular communicative intent. Authorities of the 1970s such as Carol Sager (1977) and Charles Cooper (1976) have arrived at the same conclusion: Children should write when they sense a need to write or feel a desire to write for some purpose and for some audience.

What Should Elementary School Age Children Write About?

Over the years, authorities have taken different positions concerning what topics students write about. Prior to 1917, the "accuracy movement" dominated composition instruction and attention was focused on students learning the mechanics and conventions of edited English. Predictably, students wrote on topics teachers assigned them. A 1917 report of the National Committee on the Reorganization of Secondary Schools is frequently credited with interrupting this focus and initiating a trend toward students' self-selection of their composition topics. This report, and the 1935 and 1952 reports of the Commission on the English Curriculum of NCTE, strongly influenced what came to be advocated with respect to secondary as well as elementary level composition instruction. By-words of the period were "socially relevant curricula" that placed accuracy second in importance to socially relevant writing skills and topics (National Committee on the Reorganization of Secondary Schools, 1917), "functional" or "activity curricula" (Lyman, 1932), "an experience curriculum" (Commission on the English Curriculum of NCTE, 1935), and "a life adjustment curriculum" (Hatfield, 1952).

Since the early fifties, certain movements, such as Project English in the sixties and the Back to the Basics movement in the seventies, have pulled instruction back toward more formal rhetorical study and an "accuracy" approach to composition instruction.

Accordingly, there has been less attention recently given to the importance of students selecting their own composition topics. On the other hand, emphasis on child development in the sixties and on a writing process approach to composition instruction in the seventies may serve to counter-balance the influence of such programs.

Throughout the twentieth century, authorities have also discussed the identification of topics for student writing in view of the students' stage of development. Most of the literature on the progressive stages of children's writing deals with the degree of abstraction in the content of the writing, or the degree to which the content of the writing is removed from the direct experiences of the student. Implicit in these discussions is a concern with the amount of mental maturity necessary to handle the level of abstraction of a particular writing task. Sterling Leonard (1914) has described these developmental stages as progressing from reporting observed facts, to interpreting facts; from simple to analytical expression. James Britton (1975) and Carol Burgess (1973) have noted a progression from "written down speech" that is self-expressive and includes much dialogue, to a monologue or running commentary, to a move from the expressive toward referential or transactional and poetic expression. Paul Witty and William Martin (1957) have noted that the degree of egocentricity in a piece of writing decreases as more abstract thinking increases. Time-ordered content is generally mastered before content that is not (Sterling Leonard, 1917). Experiences that prompt a piece of writing and purpose for writing also influence egocentricity and abstraction in that writing (Shirley Haley-James and David Hobson, 1980).

All of this seems to confirm the importance of students writing from their own experiences. It also suggests that students' writing about their experiences will correspond with their stage of mental development. Certainly, writing on topics that someone else has assigned and that are unrelated to personal experiences is inappropriate for students in grades one through eight.

In summation, since about 1915 the majority of authorities have pleaded the cause for students selecting composition topics drawn from their own personal experiences, perceptions, and questions. N.R. Edmund (1959) represented the position of authorities such as Lou LaBrant (1950), James Squire (1975), and James Moffett (1979) when he stated the desire to compose is born of direct and derived experiences that are meaningful to the writer; students should select their own composition topics; and topics chosen should be drawn from their experiences.

Published authors frequently acknowledge, when queried about the origin of ideas they use in their works, that they write from their personal experiences as well as the imaginings that their experiences stimulate. Those who help children with their writing may also be guided by that observation.

How Can Teachers Best Help Elementary School Age Children with Their Writing?

In a very real sense, a discussion of how teachers can help elementary age children with their writing can begin with a paraphrasing of the conclusions of preceding sections:

> Children need to write frequently about self chosen topics that are drawn from their personal experiences. If teachers set the stage for this it is likely that children will find satisfaction in communicating personal messages and information through writing. They will learn more about what they know, and reap psychological benefits of writing about what they see, feel, and experience.

Frequent writing about personally chosen topics and experiences, then, is a foundation on which teachers can build a helpful instructional program.

Guided Oral Language Processing

Many authorities stress that if children are to write about their experiences, they must learn to carefully observe those experiences and to develop clear impressions of them. They must learn to stop and see the familiar as if for the first time and be sensitive to their immediate environments. Guided oral language processing of experiences both serves this end in the immediate sense and orients children to the advantage of being alert to, and observant of, their experiences.

Alvina T. Burrows (1964, 1970) has noted that in the primary grades oral discussion of experiences is as important in the development of the ability to write as actual writing itself. The two major tasks of the primary teacher are to extend and refine oral language efficiency and build a complementary efficiency in the use of written symbols on this oral base. Both individual and group dictation of stories can be helpful in developing children's power in written language.

As early as 1900 Fred Newton Scott and Joseph V. Denny declared that student indifference to written composition is often due to the isolation of written from spoken discourse. Scott and Denny observed that oral language processing should precede, as well as occur during, children's writing. Oral language forecasting, or "prevision," is seen as a bridge to effective writing by Dora V. Smith (1946), Walter Petty et. al. (1976), and numerous other authorities who urge that teachers build a writing program on a strong oral language processing base.

The Writing Process Approach

Oral language processing that precedes and occurs during writing is also a cornerstone of the writing process approach to writing instruction. Authorities such as Sterling Leonard (1917), Ruth Carlson (1970), and Donald Murray (1973, 1978) have recommended the following steps: (1) guide children first to talk about their topics and what they want to do with them, (2) ask them to write about the topics, and (3) confer with the writers while they are writing. In the writing process approach, form is less important than ideas during the first draft.

Donald Murray (1968) has detailed what he calls the writing process "cycle of craft." It involves seven skills that writers utilize while moving through the phases of the writing process. These skills are discovering a subject, sensing an audience, searching for specifics, creating a design, writing, developing a critical eye, and re-writing. While young writers do not utilize each of these skills in every piece of writing, and other authorities might label or order the steps in variant ways, these seven skills represent "the writing process." Oral language processing with the teacher and other writers is central to a student's progression through each of these stages.

In the second stage in Murray's "cycle of craft," sensing an audience, the teacher plays a critical part in the child's identifying the audience and learning to adapt a piece of writing to that particular audience. Unless the teacher establishes through overt actions that other students as well as adults both inside and outside the school community are potential and real audiences, writing tends to become an exercise completed only as a means of fulfilling an assignment. When the teacher is the only audience for a student's writing, a sense of how to write for different audiences and purposes fails to develop.

Sterling Leonard (1917) has observed that a child writer usually begins with a general story motive, but that this may develop into other purposes and motives for writing when a child develops a sense of audience. Sensing and accommodating a particular audience is an important part of the development of any writer.

James Moffett (1968) has urged that children learn to write for audiences of four relationships: reflection (intrapersonal purpose), conversation (interpersonal, two people within close range), correspondence (interpersonal communication between remote individuals or small groups with some personal knowledge of each other), and publication (impersonal communication to larger unknown groups extended from the writer over time and space).

Alvina T. Burrows (1972) corroborates the statements of both Leonard and Moffett with the observation that there must be real, live audiences for the child's work. An enthusiastic teacher is of critical importance, but the responses of other readers and listeners are of more importance.

There is actually little literature that contradicts the concept of the writing process. Phillip Lopate (1978) does warn, however, that attention to the writing process alone will not assure growth of writing skills. The writing environment affects a student's ability to progress through the stages in the writing process, and large group environments may inhibit some students' ability to do so.

Also, some authorities have debated whether revision and refining of what has been written is more advantageous than a steady stream of new writing. The literature generally suggests that capacity for revision grows with maturity; writing purpose and a student's developing concept of audience may lead to a logical need for revising some pieces of writing; and a teacher must establish an environment conducive to students becoming absorbed enough in their work that revising for a particular communicative purpose is, at least part of the time, palatable.

Grammar and Composition

Professional literature provides very little support for the teaching of grammar in and of itself in the elementary school. More often, the recommendation has been that grammar instruction be related to, and an integral part of, revising compositions to make them appropriate for audiences who expect standard English. Young writers must work on their own oral and written language in real situations that call for good usage; they need to learn "grammar" by using language. Authorities from R. L. Lyman (1921) to those presently publishing have taken this position.

Other authorities have advocated that formal grammar instruction be undertaken in the late elementary years. However, none of these authorities has suggested that it begin before the seventh grade at which time the students' powers of abstraction are sufficient to permit them to profit from such formal grammar instruction (Carpenter et. al., 1908; Pooley, 1954 and 1958). They feel grammar study below grade eight retards natural language development and inhibits aural reception of and use of more complex language structures (Hoyt, 1906) and that even students below grade nine are not ready to undertake an analysis of someone else's language (Britton, 1970).

Some authorities have suggested alternatives to the study of formal grammar, such as sentence-combining or sentence-building games and the imitation of exemplary language heard in story telling and dramatization.

Professional references generally support the positive effect that listening to and reading good literature has on composition, but as for teachers actually using such literature as a model children can emulate, opinion is divided. Prior to 1950, it was not uncommon to see such a recommendation. However, while Hughes Mearns, who published primarily in the 1920s, and the majority of authorities publishing since 1950 have advocated exposing children to good literature, they have objected to the use of models of adult writing. They have stated that if models of good writing are used at all, the models should have been produced by other children, not adults. James Moffett (1968) and John Stewig (1980) have taken a middle-of-the-road position by recommending examples from published literature be used just to initiate writing sessions.

The literature regarding the advantage of sentence combining or sentence building exercises and games is somewhat sparse. Much of what exists is a part of research study reports, a category of professional literature not covered by this review. However, there has been authoritative support for sentence-combining reflected in the literature since at least 1917. In that year, Sterling Leonard discussed what he called sentence-massing as improving students' writing.

Sentence-massing, as defined by Leonard, involves taking two or three familiar statements that share a clear relation and combining them in various ways to show the generally superior effect of the complex form with the less important thought expressed in a phrase. Mildred Dawson (1948) said that middle-grade pupils need guidance and help in handling relationships that call for subordination of some of the clauses and help in developing more complicated ways of showing clausal relationships. She recommended sentence-combining training. James Moffett (1968), Charles Cooper (1973), and Kellogg Hunt (1977) are among other authorities who have recommended use of sentence-expansion games in middle and upper level grades.

Spelling and Composition

The literature concerning spelling instruction as it relates to the written composition program is relatively sparse. What has appeared has focused on whether words to be studied should be drawn from spelling errors that students make in their writing. Paul Klapper (1916) was one of the first twentieth-century authors to favor this approach. Words misspelled by individuals, Klapper stated, should be presented to the class, and words misspelled by the majority of the children should make up the total class spelling list. The Commission on the English Curriculum of NCTE (1935) is among those who have agreed with Klapper.

However, Harry A. Greene (1933) opposed the idea, called for more objective criteria for what is to be learned in spelling, and asked teachers to look past the present abilities and interests of students for basic units to be included in the course of study. Alvina T. Burrows (1958) urged something of a compromise by suggesting a combination of study of some of the words misspelled in children's writing and of words frequently used by children in their writing.

The late 1970s produced literature concerning spelling maturation as revealed in stages of the spelling inventions of children and implications of these stages for spelling instruction as such instruction relates to the composition program in the primary grades. J. Richard Gentry and Edmund H. Henderson (1978) urged that teachers of young children de-emphasize standard spellings; examine students' spelling for information on the quality of their knowledge of, and conceptualization of, written language; and recognize and accept nonstandard spellings that are predictable, frequent, and natural. Children need, they said, to discover relationships among spelling, meaning, and phonology, and the necessity of abstraction away from phonetic variation. Donald

Graves (1979) stated that the progression of spelling inventions and revision in beginning writers includes first inventions, words in transition, stable inventions, and sight words. Sight words are standard spellings that have stabilized. The child at the sight word stage will revise if a variant spelling is spotted. According to Graves, spelling will develop along these stages if children are encouraged to write and spell freely.

The Classroom Teacher and Composition

The data related to the importance of (a) the teacher including frequent writing on student chosen topics, (b) oral language processing before and during writing, and (c) building a composition program around a writing process approach are relatively clear. We can likewise draw certain conclusions from the literature regarding how grammar instruction and spelling may be handled.

There are other aspects of the teacher's job that are also mentioned in the literature, however. The importance of the teacher *being* a writer is one of these. Lou LaBrant (1955), Donald Murray (1978), and Donald Graves (1978) are representative of authorities who have stressed that the effective teacher of writing at any level is a writer, not just a critic of students' writing.

The teacher's having a positive attitude toward, and high expectations for, every student writer is also important (Cooper, 1976). Most authorities agree that the teacher's attitude strongly influences student writers.

How Can Teachers Best Evaluate the Writing of Elementary School Age Children?

The professional literature on methods used from 1900 through 1979 to evaluate student writing is more trend-related than much of the other literature on writing. Though one method has never been used exclusively, there have been times when one approach has been quite evidently dominant.

From 1900 to the early forties, for instance, rating scales were the most commonly advocated means of measuring the quality of student writing. Edward L. Thorndike (1911) and M. B. Hillegas (1912), convinced that scales for accurately evaluating writing could be devised and the value of a student's theme could be derived through statistical analysis, worked individually and cooperatively on what ultimately became the Hillegas-Thorndike Scales. E. C. Noyes (1912) subsequently declared that the writing samples in the Hillegas-Thorndike Scale (to which teachers were to compare their students' compositions) were too long, but conceded that Hillegas had shown that standardized measurement of composition quality was possible.

For the next several years various scholars applied their energies to improving upon the quality of the information obtained from the use of rating scales. Frank W. Ballou (1914), E. Hudelson (1916), S. B. Breed and F. W. Frostic (1917), and M. R. Trabue (1917) worked on variation in teacher judgments of the quality of student writing in relation to pieces of writing that made up the scales and on standardizing the distance between scale compositions.

In 1917, references to the limitations of rating scales began to appear with greater frequency than they had previously. M. R. Trabue (1917) warned that rating scales could only safely be used to compare *classes* of composition students on the same grade level. A single rated composition is not sufficient, he observed, for judging how a student writes because the rating process is subject to errors of judgment on individual pieces.

Sterling Leonard (1919) further cautioned that if scales were used, all students who were writing should write on one topic and only teachers carefully trained to use a given scale should use it. Finally, Hudelson (1921) reversed his previously "pro" stance on the use of writing scales because of the unequal steps between scale compositions and problems in scale and rater reliability. From that point on, much of the literature regarding the use of rating scales for evaluating student compositions expressed, at best, tentative support for their use, and by the 1940s their use had for the most part been abandoned.

Professional literature from the mid-forties to the seventies suggests that a variety of evaluation methods were used and debate waged related primarily to the "red ink blitz" phenomenon. Teachers and other scholars argued for sitting down and showing a student what was wrong with a piece of work; for not grading a student's work at all; and for clearer standards for successful writing.

The term *holistic evaluation* emerged as a by-word in the 1970s. Holistic evaluation generally involved a quick, general impression reading, whether for a specific feature in the writing as in primary trait scoring, or for the purpose of attaining a global impression of the entire piece. Richard Lloyd-Jones (1977) described holistic evaluation as generally more valid, more informative, and more expensive than other means of evaluation.

Charles Cooper (1977) refers to holistic evaluation as a guided procedure for sorting and ranking pieces of writing. No enumerating of or tallying of a feature, even when a particular feature is the focus of attention, is undertaken. Instead, the rater makes judgments about the presence or absence of the feature of the writing that is being evaluated. Cooper's interpretation of holistic evaluation procedures bears some resemblance, in the scaling sense, to rating scales used from 1910 to 1930.

Teacher and peer conferences with student writers became the most prominently recommended method of evaluating writing by the mid 1970s. In a writing conference situation, the writer is always present when the teacher or another student writer responds to and comments on a student's paper (Squire, 1975). Charles Cooper (1977) urged that in a writing conference the person giving the conference focus on getting the writer to identify only a few problems that most need attention, to leave editorial problems to the last stage of revision, and to understand what is necessary to improve the paper.

Positive feedback is an important part of the writing conference. Donald Graves (1978) recommends that after several pieces of work have been completed the teacher meet with the student and select the best pieces in the student's writing folder. Students often gain insight through this procedure into what worked best for them and set goals to work toward in future pieces of writing.

Donald Murray (1979), perhaps the most widely published authority on the writing conference approach to evaluating writing, recommends that writing conferences be used at all grade levels and all levels of writing proficiency.

Observations Drawn From This Review of Professional Literature

The opinion of any one authority may or may not impress us as credible. We assess a particular authority's credibility in the context of what we ourselves have experienced and observed and in the light of what other authorities tell us. When numerous authorities agree on a point, however, that at least causes us to pause and reflect about what they recommend.

Not all of those cited in this review of authoritative opinion agreed with one another. The strength of their agreement or disagreement varied with the topic and sometimes with the time periods in which they worked. There were, on the other hand, certain points on which numerous authorities agreed, and the strength of their agreement seems to warrant making the following observations about writing instruction and writing programs in grades one through eight.

Children learn to write by writing.

Even very young school age children whose knowledge of letter formations and spelling patterns is limited can and should write.

Writing frequently on self-selected topics is important to developing skill in writing.

When children feel a need or a desire to write for some purpose or audience, they write more effectively.

Children should write from their experiences, and expectations for their writing should be in line with their stage of experiential and mental development.

Oral language processing of the ideas and content being expressed should precede writing and occur during writing.

Real and varied audiences for their work are important to the development of children as writers and to their incentive to write.

Writing purpose and a developing concept of audience lead children to a logical need for revising selected pieces of their writing.

Formal study of grammar should be delayed until grade eight or nine; until then revising writing in view of the audience for the writing should be the basis of grammar-related language study.

Teacher and peer conferences with the writer are appropriate means of helping children process their writing orally and progress from first drafts, in which primary concern is with getting meaning out on paper, to improved drafts.

Holistic and primary trait scoring are useful means of assessing both the progress of groups of children and the effectiveness of writing programs.

How These Observations Relate to the Remainder of This Book

These eleven observations have been drawn from points that numerous cited authorities have agreed upon. These same observations are reflected in the writing programs and teaching practices described in Chapters 3 through 6 of this monograph. They relate closely as well to the contents of Chapter 7, which deals with changes in writing research that will be needed if writing research is to constructively affect writing instruction. In their aggregate, these observations about effective writing instruction represent a philosophical framework within which the contents of the entire monograph can be examined.

The second chapter is made up of data gleaned from a random survey of teaching practices of a sample classroom of fourth-grade teachers. These data provide a perspective on changes that improved composition instruction in grades one through eight may require.

Classroom Teachers' Reports on Teaching Written Composition

Walter T. Petty
State University of New York, Amherst

Patrick J. Finn
State University of New York, Buffalo

Public and professional concern about the teaching of written composition leads to the question of how it is being taught; more specifically, how it is being taught in elementary schools. This, of course, is a question that is impossible to answer briefly, simply, or with a great deal of assurance. There are too many classrooms and there is too much variance in the personalities, beliefs, and knowledge of teachers. However, the NCTE Committee on Teaching Written Composition in Elementary Schools was charged to "survey written composition teaching practices in a nationally distributed sample of elementary schools." Thus, the Executive Committee of NCTE assumed that at least some information could be gained about elementary composition teaching, and this chapter reviews answers gained by means of a questionnaire (see Figure 1 at the end of this chapter) to such questions as: How much time do you devote to teaching written composition? How frequently do children write? What means are used to interest them in writing? What forms of writing are taught? What specific teaching practices do you use? What are children's major writing problems?

Developing and Distributing the Questionnaire

The questionnaire was developed in early 1977 and was distributed in two phases—one in the latter part of 1977 and the other in March of 1978.[1] The first distribution, approximately 1400 questionnaires, was made to teachers in many parts of the country by

---

1. The questionnaire was developed by the authors and Dr. Jean Peek, Language Arts Coordinator of the Williamsville Schools, New York, but members of the committee provided suggestions for revising the first drafts.

members of the committee and by colleagues who are members of NCTE. However, this distribution was not a truly nationally distributed sample, nor were some controls applied that are desirable in questionnaire surveys. Thus, the first distribution was regarded as a pilot study, but it did prove that the questionnaire was reasonable, and it provided the opportunity for validating responses and for making minor changes in the wording of a few questions. Of the 1400 initially distributed, 886 questionnaires were returned.

The second distribution was made to 1000 fourth-grade teachers and is the basis of this report. The tabulations of the findings appear in Figure 1 at the end of this chapter. Although the committee recognized that teaching practices may differ from grade level to grade level, the members agreed that the responses of fourth-grade teachers would supply reasonable evidence of the teaching practices of elementary school teachers in general. The teachers for this distribution were selected at random from lists of fourth-grade teachers in each state. The number sent the questionnaire in each state was determined by calculating what percentage the number of teachers on the state list was of the total number of teachers.[2] Stamped envelopes for returning the questionnaires were supplied and a cut-off date for their return was established. Three hundred and nineteen questionnaires were returned by that date. Because of limited resources, no follow-up was made in this distribution to seek a higher return. The higher percentage of returned questionnaires in the first distribution was likely due to the follow-up efforts of the NCTE members who distributed the questionnaires in their locales.

The Validity of Questionnaire Responses

The issue of validity is always present in questionnaire research, since consideration must be given to such questions as: Do respondents understand the questions in the same way as the question writers? Do the respondents answer the questions accurately? Do those who return the questionnaire fairly represent those who did

---

2. Names and home addresses of the teachers were obtained from Market Data Retrieval of Westport, CT. This organization had available the names and addresses of 977,143 elementary school teachers listed by states. Thus, to determine the number of teachers in a state to receive the questionnaire, the number of teachers in Alabama, for example (16,161), was calculated to be 1.7 percent of the total. Therefore, a random selection of seventeen fourth-grade Alabama teachers were sent the questionnaire. The number of teachers who were sent and who returned questionnaires in each state is given in Figure 2 at the end of the chapter.

not respond or those who were not asked to? These questions, of course, can seldom, if ever, be answered completely in questionnaire research.

In the questionnaire, one question asked whether or not parallel structure is a problem in teaching written composition. One teacher wrote, "I don't know what parallel structure means, so I don't think it's a problem." This is an extreme case, but it did cause us to wonder how frequently the teachers chose answers when they were aware that they did not understand the question. The opposite creates a problem as well—respondents think that they understand a question, but don't understand it in the way the writer intended. For example, in the first distribution of the questionnaire, when asked to what extent they use adults as writing models for their students, more kindergarten and first-grade teachers indicated that such models were used frequently than did teachers in grades two through five. Thus, we suspected that these kindergarten and first-grade teachers were thinking of stories dictated by children but written by the teacher as "using an adult model."

The problem of whether what a respondent indicates as practice in the classroom actually occurs is not necessarily a question of respondents answering falsely, although one teacher wrote:

> When answering this survey, a twinge of conscience tempted me to check the next higher choice. I gave in to it several times.

Most discrepancy between responses and actual practice is more likely a matter of the accuracy of a teacher's perceptions or in making distinctions in the meanings of the choices open to them than it is of honesty. We know that our perceptions of many things change from day to day; therefore, any teacher might have answered some questions differently if the questionnaire had been responded to on another day. On the other hand, these differences are likely to be minor ones in an over-all sense. A teacher who evaluates children's writing in a particular way might choose "frequently" one day and "almost always" another, but is not likely to change from one of these choices to "never."

In our opinion, the number of responses to the first distribution of the questionnaire (886), and the follow-ups made by the district and college or university personnel making the distribution, reduced the likelihood of wide discrepancies in responses that might occur if data were available from those fourth-grade teachers who did not respond. This seems particularly rational because of the close correspondence of the responses in the first distribution to those made by the fourth-grade teachers in the structured sample.

As to the other validity problems, the responses of twenty-five of the teachers in the first distribution were verified by district supervisory personnel. In addition, the responses of another forty teachers (who signed their questionnaires) were verified by college or university teachers who knew the respondents and their teaching practices well. This verification provides some evidence of validity, but because of the general problems of survey research of the type we did, as well as our inability to extend the verification, we do not present these findings as a necessarily accurate picture of teaching practices. Furthermore, the nature of the questionnaire—particularly not forcing the teachers to rank practices in terms of their use—makes interpretation of the findings difficult. We do believe, however, that the high percentages of responses to many of the questions provides reasonable evidence about many practices.

Demographic Data about Respondents

The majority of the fourth-grade teachers (51.6 percent) had been teaching from six to fifteen years, 34 percent had earned master's degrees, and the overwhelming majority of the majors for this degree (74.5 percent) was elementary education. The respondents were female at a ratio of nine to one.

As to the type of school in which they were teaching, more than 95 percent of the teachers identified it as an elementary school (rather than middle or intermediate), and the most common combination of grades in the schools (43.2 percent) was kindergarten through grade six. Almost 35 percent of the respondents taught in schools with student populations of 400 to 599. The most common class-size range was twenty-five to twenty-nine (40.7 percent), but more than 22 percent of the teachers were teaching classes of thirty or more students. The large majority of these fourth-grade teachers (71.7 percent) were teaching in self-contained classrooms.

Summary of the Findings

An overwhelming majority of the teachers (86.6 percent) reported spending at least thirty minutes daily teaching language arts. Over 25 percent spend more than sixty minutes. Just what this latter response means, however, is not clear; are these teachers teaching language arts all day long or do they have a language arts period that is longer than sixty minutes?

Apparently the largest share of the language arts instructional time (the questionnaire asked the time devoted to reading be excluded in responding) is given to written expression, but with grammar and spelling given almost as much time. The amount of time given to these three areas means that little time is given to dramatics (69.5 percent of the teachers reported "less than 5 percent") and speech (46.8 percent reported "less than 5 percent"). Listening and handwriting apparently receive more attention than do speech and dramatics but considerably less than writing, grammar, and spelling.

Almost half of the teachers reported that children in their classes write daily, although the frequency that children apparently do grammar and mechanics exercises may suggest that some of the daily "writing" is of the exercise nature. However, since fill-in-the-blanks writing was not a choice, the respondents identified the forms of most of this writing as stories, personal experience narratives, summaries and reports, and descriptions. Relatively little instructional attention is apparently given to personal or social letter writing (59.8 percent indicated that they "never" or "seldom" gave it instructional attention) and even less to the writing of business letters (86.4 percent said either "never" or "seldom"). Other forms that children do not write in very often include essays, directions, news articles, and announcements.

Most frequently being used to stimulate writing were pictures, objects, discussions, topics, and stories. Television was infrequently or never used, and the same was generally true for music, sensory experiences, and dramatics.

The practices reported as being used frequently were led by "having students do punctuation and capitalization exercises" (52.8 percent indicated that these are used "almost always" and 43.7 percent reported their use "frequently") and · "requiring completion of grammar exercises" (52.4 percent said "almost always" and 40.6 percent said "frequently"). "Allowing children to cross out, insert, etc., on first draft" is a practice indicated as being followed "frequently" or "almost always" (a total of 86.2 percent). Encouraging nonassigned writing was reported as a "frequently" or "almost always" used practice by nearly 75 percent of the teachers; however, "providing time and place for unassigned writing" was reported as "never" or "seldom" by more than 45 percent of the respondents.

The responses also showed some possible contradictions in practices. For example, such opposing practices as that of spelling words orally for children and those of writing spelling words on slips of paper or on the board were all reported as being used "frequently." However, "sending children to the dictionary for spelling help" was identified as being practiced even more frequently.

Some discrepancy may also be reflected in the fact that both giving a single letter or numerical grade and assigning separate grades for content and mechanics were both practices having high percentages of "frequently" and "almost always" responses. The teachers reported that they "frequently" or "almost always" comment on compositional aspects of pupils' writing (93.4 percent combined). Approximately the same was reported in regard to commenting about mechanical aspects of writing.

Only about 45 percent of teachers indicated that they "frequently" or "almost always" evaluate writing products "according to previously established standards," and even fewer use a scale or checklist in evaluation. A rather large percentage of the teachers (76.7 percent) at least frequently "have individual conferences with children."

In line with the apparent teaching emphasis on grammar, punctuation, and capitalization, more than 75 percent of the fourth-grade teachers reported that they "frequently" or "almost always" gave objective tests over these aspects of their programs.

The aspects of written composition reported as being serious instructional problems were "run-ons," "sentence fragments," and "limited or trite vocabulary." As one might have predicted spelling, punctuation, capitalization, and organization were identified as "often a problem." Choosing appropriate content for the expression was the aspect least regarded as a problem. This was followed by "inappropriate word choices." We regarded "inappropriate word choices" as the bulk of the departures from "standard" usage. Possibly many of the teachers did not have the same understanding. Yet the study showed that high percentages of teachers apparently regard agreement of pronoun with antecedent and nonstandard verb choices as often or occasionally a problem.

Because the teachers who returned the questionnaire teach in all sections of the country and differ in the number of years that they have taught as well as other factors, we tabulated the responses in terms of a number of these variables to gain some idea of the effects of these differences upon the findings. We did not attempt a statistical analysis because of the complexity of the design of the questionnaire (i.e. the range in possible responses to questions, the imprecision in meaning of such terms as "frequently," "seldom," etc., and the tabulation of responses in percentages) but by inspection of the totals of the "never" and "seldom" response percentages as compared to those of "frequently" and "almost always," some differences became apparent in regard to several of the variables.

For example, the teachers with more than ten years experience devote less of their language arts program time to spelling, grammar, and listening and slightly more time to speech than do teachers with less experience. There is also a tendency for the teachers with less experience to use individual conferences in evaluating writing more often than do their more experienced counterparts. The more experienced teachers frequently use virtually all of the means the questionnaire implies as being useful for stimulating writing. It appears that the less experienced teachers have a smaller repertory of such techniques. Other differences related to the experience variable were negligible.

Differences in the responses of teachers whose highest degree is the bachelor's compared with those holding the master's or higher degree were generally minimal. Exceptions are that the teachers with a master's degree or higher are definitely more inclined to use field trips to stimulate writing, to have the children do more news writing, and to permit children to cross out and insert in their writing than are the teachers with bachelor's degrees. The teachers with the bachelor's as their highest degree showed a slight tendency to consider double negatives, nonstandard verbs, and improper word choices to be more serious problems than did the teachers with the advanced degrees.

More time was devoted to teaching grammar by the teachers who had majored in English than by those with other majors. The English majors also regarded limiting the subject, outlining, organization, and improper word choices as more serious problems than did the teachers with other majors. In fact, in contrast with the responses of those with other majors, not one of the teachers with English majors regarded any of the grammar, sentence, or composition items as "no problem."

The male teachers in the study (10 percent of the sample) give somewhat more of their language arts program time to written composition than the female teachers do. The male teachers also give more attention to essay and news writing, but slightly less to poetry, and they are also less likely to give separate grades for content and mechanics.

We grouped the responses of teachers by states (forty-eight states were represented in the returns) into five groups: northeast, southeast, central, southwest, and far west. Some of the differences are interesting but, of course, dividing 319 responses into five segments reduces one's confidence about concluding very much concerning practices of teachers in the areas. The comparison did show that 50 percent of the teachers in the southeast devote 10 percent or less of their language arts program time to written composition while only 30 percent of teachers in the other areas reported that small a percentage. The teachers in the southeast, as well as those in the southwest, tend to regard changes in tense, improper word choices, double negatives, and nonstandard verbs as greater problems than do the teachers in the other regions. Teachers in the northeast give somewhat more instructional attention to letter writing—both personal and business—and to essay writing than do the other teachers. They are also less inclined to give single letter grades on writing products. The teachers in the far west responding to the questionnaire, on the other hand, appear to use more techniques in evaluation that we would label as "traditional." That is, they are less inclined to assign grades related to the writer's ability or improvement and to use pupil self-evaluation.

The comparisons that we made of responses related to other variables—number of students in class, school, or district; type of school; or number of classes taught per day—showed negligible differences.

Discussion of the Results

On the basis of this survey, it seems fair to conclude that teachers have largely incorporated into their classrooms the techniques that have been suggested by language arts specialists in recent decades for stimulating or motivating children to write. We were somewhat surprised to find that television was so little used in motivating writing, but this is probably accounted for by the fact that few specialists have been very specific in their suggestions about its use. The emphasis of recent years on "creative writing" is also reflected in the responses, since the forms most often thought of as creative are those in which children most often write.

The recent emphasis on "basics" is possibly reflected in the high percentage of language arts program time given to grammar and mechanics exercises and to the testing done in these areas as well as by the relatively little time devoted to speech activities. On the other hand, perhaps the traditional emphasis is simply still being given in classrooms, since some writing forms that one might consider to be basic—letter writing, for instance—receive little attention. Probably definitions of "the basics" are as varied among these teachers as they are among most professional and lay people alike. It is obvious, though, that many of the teachers responding to the questionnaire are very concerned about the teaching of spelling and other elements of mechanics and convention. Yet there does not appear to be the emphasis on using checklists and established standards in evaluation that might be expected to result from this concern.

Since the study indicated that considerable time is generally given to the teaching of written composition, it would seem reasonable to expect more instructional attention to be given to a number of forms of writing than is apparently the case. Supporting this expectation, too, is the report that children write rather frequently. However, as indicated earlier in this report, we wonder what this writing is. Is much of it the filling in of the blanks and the like, or is it largely writing stories and personal experience accounts? The fact that comparatively little instructional attention appears to be given to a number of writing forms, as well as to some elements important to composition, leads us to conclude that much of the time given to teaching writing does not focus on written expression as one ordinarily thinks of it.

1. Years of teaching experience:
   1   2.2   6-15   51.6   over 20   16.0
   2-5   16.4   16-20   13.8

2. Highest degree earned:
   bachelor's   62.7   sixth year certificate   2.8
   master's   34.2   doctorate   0.0
                                none   0.3

3. Academic major of highest degree:
   Elementary Education 74.5   Elementary Educ./English   3.8
   Secondary Education   1.3   Secondary Educ./English   0.3
   General Education   3.1   Reading   3.1
   English   1.6   none of above   12.3

4. Type of school:
   elementary   95.3
   intermediate   3.5
   middle   0.2

5. Combination of grades in the school:
   K-5   21.5   1-6   6.9
   K-6   43.2   1-8   0.3
   K-8   10.1   4-6   7.6
   1-5   9.8   4-9   0.6

6. Number of students in the school:
   < 100   2.2   200-399   23.8   600-799   21.3
   100-199   10.8   400-599   34.9   800-999   3.5
                                                over 1000   3.5

7. Number of students in classes:
   5-14   2.8   20-24   26.8   30-34   19.2
   15-19   7.3   25-29   40.7   35-40   2.2
                                           > 40   0.9

8. The term that best describes the teaching situation:
   self-contained classroom   71.7
   team teaching   13.2
   departmentalization   9.9
   other (individualized, open education, etc.)   5.2

9. Number of classroom groups taught writing daily:
   one   69.9   four   3.2
   two   17.0   five   2.6
   three   5.1   > five   2.2

Figure 1. Responses of 319 fourth-grade teachers to questions concerning their language arts programs and practices in the teaching of written composition. Responses are given as a percentage of the teachers who gave that response.

10. Minutes per day devoted to language arts instruction, excluding reading:

< 15 minutes	0.3	46-60 minutes	33.1
15-30 minutes	13.1	> 60 minutes	25.8
31-45 minutes	27.7		

11. Amount of time in language arts programs devoted to various language arts areas (other than reading):

	< 5%	5% -10%	10%-25%	25%-50%	> 50%
spelling	3.2	20.3	45.5	28.7	2.3
handwriting	24.4	39.4	31.1	4.8	0.3
dramatics	69.5	22.5	6.3	1.6	0.0
grammar	3.5	17.7	35.8	33.9	9.2
written composition	5.0	28.1	39.4	24.9	2.5
speech	46.8	31.0	17.1	4.7	0.3
listening	16.1	41.5	29.7	10.4	2.2

12. Frequency of student writing:

daily	49.2	two or more times weekly	28.6
weekly	15.9	bi-weekly	4.8

13. The extent that each of the following is used to stimulate children to write:

	never	seldom	frequently	almost always
movies	14.2	59.2	25.6	0.9
television	30.7	50.0	19.0	0.3
filmstrips or slides	11.4	45.3	39.6	3.8
pictures	3.8	27.8	62.3	6.0
other objects	7.2	35.9	50.0	6.9
music	28.5	56.0	14.6	0.9
whole class discussion	2.5	16.6	56.7	24.1
small group discussion	9.8	36.1	45.9	8.2
dramatics	27.5	50.3	19.9	2.2
field trips	17.6	48.1	29.9	4.4
a topic or title	1.6	17.4	63.7	17.4
beginning sentence	5.7	27.8	56.5	10.1
story or narrative setting	3.5	33.4	54.6	8.5
brainstorming ideas	9.5	38.3	43.7	8.5
reading a story or poem	5.1	32.0	56.3	6.6
sensory experiences	15.5	45.9	33.9	4.7

Figure 1. Continued.

14. The frequency that students write in the following forms:

	never	seldom	frequently	almost always
personal or social letters	1.3	58.5	38.7	1.6
business letters	26.6	59.5	13.0	0.9
stories	1.9	10.1	63.5	24.5
summaries and reports	4.1	30.1	55.2	10.7
descriptions	4.1	32.0	56.3	7.6
directions	10.1	58.7	27.4	3.8
news writing	21.2	55.1	19.0	4.7
poetry	4.7	45.8	44.8	4.7
essays	18.2	46.5	31.4	3.8
announcements and notices	23.6	64.2	11.6	0.6
personal experience narratives	2.5	18.6	62.9	16.0

15. The frequency that the following are practiced:

	never	seldom	frequently	almost always
listing words on the board which may be spelling problems	6.0	24.4	49.2	20.3
writing requested spelling words on slips of paper	9.8	24.4	42.0	23.3
sending children to dictionary for spelling help	1.6	14.8	48.7	34.9
spelling words orally when spelling help is requested	4.7	28.8	48.0	18.5
allowing children to cross out, insert, etc. on first draft	4.4	9.5	37.9	48.3
requiring rewriting (copy over)	1.6	17.6	47.8	33.0
using the writing of other students as models	11.7	45.7	37.9	4.7
having children read their writing aloud to the class	1.9	20.1	62.4	15.7
posting selected writing on bulletin boarrd	5.3	23.2	54.2	17.2
using adults' writing as models	34.0	44.0	18.9	3.1
assigning writing in connection with other subject areas	1.6	12.5	65.2	20.8
encouraging non-assigned writing	4.1	23.3	52.1	20.5
providing time and place for unassigned writing	11.3	34.3	37.7	16.7

Figure 1. Continued.

allowing children to ask peers for help	0.6	19.7	51.4	28.3
requiring completion of grammar exercises	0.6	6.3	40.6	52.4
having students do punctuation and capitalization exercises	0.9	2.5	43.7	52.8
developing a paragraph or story as a group activity	7.2	37.7	39.9	15.1

16. The extent to which these practices are used in evaluating children's writing:

	never	seldom	frequently	almost always
assign a single letter or numerical grade	27.1	22.0	33.1	17.8
assign separate grades for content and mechanics	26.4	28.3	32.8	12.5
comment on mechanical items needing improvement	1.6	8.3	52.7	36.9
comment on compositional items needing improvement (organization, sentence structure, etc.)	2.5	10.1	51.6	35.8
comment on mechanical aspects that are especially good or show improvement	0.3	6.0	48.9	44.8
comment on compositional aspects that are well done or show improvement	0.0	6.6	46.4	47.0
have individual conferences with children	1.3	22.0	45.6	31.1
have group evaluation by students	30.8	47.2	19.8	2.2
have each child evaluate own writing	12.3	39.9	38.7	8.9
have another teacher evaluate writing	65.3	27.8	6.3	0.6
evaluate by a teacher team	79.7	16.5	3.8	0.0
evaluate according to previously established standards	24.5	30.3	36.9	8.3
use a scale or checklist	38.3	36.3	21.2	4.2
give objective tests on punctuation and capitalization	3.2	17.4	54.4	25.0
give objective tests on grammar	4.4	16.7	53.3	25.6

Figure 1. Continued.

evaluate only selected pieces of writing	22.9	33.1	36.6	7.3
assign grade depending on student's ability	13.5	10.6	40.8	35.0
assign grade according to individual improvement	11.0	10.6	50.0	28.4

17. The extent the following are considered to be written composition problems for students:

	not a problem	occasionally a problem	often a problem	a serious problem	attention not given to this item
legibility of handwriting	6.7	47.3	37.1	8.6	0.3
spelling	1.6	26.6	54.9	16.6	0.3
capitalization	3.5	35.8	49.1	11.6	0.0
punctuation	0.9	29.2	53.3	16.6	0.0
agreement of subject and verb	5.4	40.4	40.1	9.1	5.0
agreement of pronoun with antecedent	7.6	36.3	28.3	8.3	19.4
non-standard verb forms	3.0	33.8	34.8	12.8	15.7
double negatives	9.5	37.1	30.8	16.5	6.0
improper word choices (other than verbs)	4.8	42.2	36.7	11.8	4.5
changes in tense	2.2	29.5	49.7	14.7	3.8
sentence fragments	2.5	24.6	43.2	26.5	3.2
run-ons	1.9	13.9	40.5	37.7	6.0
misplaced modifiers	6.2	30.5	28.2	7.5	27.5
awkward constructions	2.3	27.1	38.4	19.4	12.9
parallel structure	3.7	19.3	25.1	5.1	46.8
redundancy	3.2	24.6	33.3	12.9	25.9
varied sentence structure	1.3	22.7	35.4	12.3	28.2
outlining	2.9	18.3	31.1	14.7	33.0
limiting the subject	6.1	28.5	36.6	10.4	18.4
organization	1.9	21.7	50.8	18.5	7.0
limited or trite vocabulary	2.3	22.9	44.8	21.9	8.1
developing ideas	4.2	25.6	49.2	16.0	5.1
supporting opinions	3.2	20.9	28.0	13.5	34.4
choosing appropriate or interesting content	9.7	34.3	37.5	11.0	7.4
rewriting and revising	5.8	29.2	39.4	17.0	8.7

Figure 1. Continued.

	Number sent[*]	Number returned		Number sent[*]	Number returned
Alabama	17	3	Missouri	22	6
Alaska	2	1	Montana	4	3
Arizona	11	1	Nebraska	8	5
Arkansas	9	4	Nevada	3	1
California	97	25	New Hampshire	4	2
Colorado	12	4	New Jersey	36	8
Connecticut	16	6	New Mexico	6	1
Delaware	3	0	New York	79	19
District of Columbia	4	2	North Carolina	28	7
			North Dakota	3	1
Florida	34	10	Ohio	48	19
Georgia	25	9	Oklahoma	14	8
Hawaii	5	2	Oregon	12	7
Idaho	4	3	Pennsylvania	41	16
Illinois	55	21	Rhode Island	4	1
Indiana	25	8	South Carolina	14	3
Iowa	14	2	South Dakota	4	1
Kansas	12	5	Tennessee	20	3
Kentucky	16	3	Texas	61	19
Louisiana	19	7	Utah	6	3
Maine	6	3	Vermont	3	3
Maryland	17	6	Virginia	24	5
Massachusetts	28	9	Washington	16	6
Michigan	44	15	West Virginia	10	1
Minnesota	19	6	Wisconsin	21	10
Mississippi	13	6	Wyoming	2	0

[*]Number sent based on percent of total U.S. elementary school teachers in that state.

Figure 2. Number of questionnaires sent out and returned.

A "Whole-Language Approach" Writing Program

Vera Milz
Bloomfield Hills School District, Michigan

Helping children write well has been a major concern of schools for many years. I share this concern each year as I am faced with the challenge of my own primary teaching assignment.

Looking back over the years recently, I realized that children had always written notes and stories that amused and interested me. They had often used creative spellings that I had not taught them. Christmas had become a particularly pleasant time, as many children continued to write to me though they were no longer in my class.

As I became aware of the exciting research of educators and linguists in the field of child language development, this information began to give me new insight into what had been and was happening to learners in my classroom. I began to question some of my practices, to shift some of my priorities, and to look more closely at the children in my classroom as they began to write. Once I focused on them as learners and realized the potential for composing in first and second grade children, I could choose materials and plan activities that would enhance their natural tendencies as language users. As a result, the children began to write sooner and more often than in previous years. The notes, journal entries, letters, stories, and poems that have since emerged have supported my belief that children *want* to communicate in writing.

Language Knowledge

Linguists maintain that by age five most children orally learn their native language (Cazden, 1969). They are surrounded by speech from the day of their birth. Gradually, they learn to communicate and by school age they can carry on a meaningful conversation with peers and adults. Speech is learned holistically in a social context. Children have not been given special exercises to help them develop their speech, but instead they have learned naturally and easily as they have felt the need to communicate.

A six-year-old learning English several days after leaving his home in Indonesia illustrated this point in my classroom. One of the first words he spoke after his second day in school was *milk* as he presented me with his dime at lunchtime. We took the dime to the place where he could purchase milk for his lunch. At the end of the day, he went to a classroom chart and read orally *2 Blue*, under which his name had been printed. It had been a long day; Francis was ready to go home, and he knew the 2 Blue bus would take him there.

Language in Action

In our literate society, productive forms of language—speech and writing—exist side by side along with the receptive forms, listening and reading. All are mutually supportive in the classroom and do not develop alone; the listener responds to the speaker while the reader reads what the writer has written. Researchers Kenneth and Yetta Goodman (1976) believe that "children learn to read and write in the same way and for the same reason that they learn to speak and listen."

Francis provided an example of the way the language processes interact. When Heather protested she could not open her milk carton, he frantically began to point out her problem. She had not used the side that said *open*. He did not have enough control of the English language to explain this, but already he could read the word, understand its meaning, and try to help another child understand. By the time the incident ended, he could also say *open*.

Writing must be an integral useful part of the classroom and be related to the child's individual needs. Francis quickly read his name labels on his possessions, such as a supply can and a coat hook. When I told him he could take a book home and showed him he could put it in his tote bag, he pulled out a pencil and wrote *Francis* across the cover.

To further demonstrate the relationships between the oral and written language processes, the technique described by Barry Sherman (1979 p.43) as "written conversation" is a useful starting point:

> Write a message to a child, read it aloud as the child looks on, and then hand paper and pencil to the child for a response. If the child says, "I can't write," respond with "Just pretend to write, then tell me what you want to say." (Sometimes both teacher and child read their messages aloud as they write.)

Amazingly, few children write nothing. They know how to talk and their writing is easily related to what they already know. An early conversation may look like this:

Teacher: Hi
Child: Hi
Teacher: I am Miss Milz
Child: I am Greg
Teacher: I like dogs
Child: I like U
Teacher: I like you, too.

Getting Started with Writing

Writing serves a legitimate function in a child's personal and social life; it grows because of what it has to do. Speech is learned in a communication situation with persons sharing a meaningful and relevant context. Writing must also deal with real situations and subjects about which children wish to communicate. Topics must be those students are interested in. Don Graves (1973) reports that giving students the choice of subject has a tremendous effect on the amount and quality of their writing.

Children also need understanding teachers who will share experiences with them. A beginning speaker is surrounded by adults eager to respond. Halliday (1975) noted that his son at eighteen months had no conception of language as a means of communicating an experience to someone who had not shared that experience with him. When Nigel said *syrup*, it took parents sharing that experience to know it meant "I want my syrup." Beginning writers need the same support. Paul was tired of being ignored by a busy mother. He tossed her a note that had R U DF printed on it. His mother got the message (Bissex, 1979).

Beginning writers sometimes forget their message and it is only the encouraging response of the understanding recipient who reads the message that seems to get them to try again. Initially,

many beginners ask for every letter in a word, so it is important
to see them move to writing more independently. These two
samples show the change in Tagg and reflect his growing knowledge
from the first week in first grade to the end of the month as he
wrote me several notes.

September 8   September 30

MISS MILZ   Dear Miss milZ
I LIKE   I THk THeT YOU
BEING   ARE NSH THR
IN YOUR   Love tagg
CLASS.

TAGG

As his teacher, it was easy for me to read both of his notes. Many
of his journal entries were also about things that happened to both
of us in the same classroom.

Functional Writing Activities

Once children are identified in my class membership, I send a wel-
coming letter to each of them. In the letter, I invite them to stop
by to meet me while I am setting up the classroom. When they
arrive, I show them their mailbox and mine. Children are introduced to the usefulness of written language even if they can't read
the letter. Within days, I am receiving notes and these messages are
exchanged all year long.

                                        June 16

Dear MiSS Mills   Dear Miss Milz,
tabay IS the Lat   Today is the last
bay for Schol   day of school.
I Will *Miss. MiSS*   I will miss Miss
MilS MayB che *May*   Milz. Maybe she may
MiSS Me   miss me.
        Chip   Chip

Notes can be extended beyond the classroom. Children need
to extend their audience beyond a teacher. When I suggest to
parents that they put a note in a lunchbox, many do so and are
pleased to find a note returned by the child. Penpals are easy to
find. This year my class is writing letters to England, Canada, and
Virginia. Their penpals range from first graders to sixth graders.

Each time a new set of letters arrives, they are eagerly answered. I am seeing my first graders change as they answer each set, and they are learning how to write letters as they actually do it. The ending *Yours Truly* is now being used by many of the children in the following ways: yous truly, url frad shole, Your truly friend.

During the first week of school each child is given a spiral notebook to be used as a personal journal. This notebook is to be used as the child wishes, and each day I read it and respond in writing if appropriate. My responses are directed to the meaning, and I do not correct the child's writing. Topics arise naturally as we explore the content areas of the curriculum. I ask the children to date each entry they make, so at the beginning of the school year I record the date on the chalkboard along with relevant classroom news. Soon children take over the task. When children couldn't remember what days special classes were, they were asked to record them on the calendar.

Monday	Tuesday	Wednesday	Thursday	Friday
Nothing	Gym	Music	Gym	Music
	Art			Gym

Several children wrote the schedule in their personal journals.

Holidays are a frequent choice of subject by young children. For example, Donald wrote his Christmas list in his journal:

December 7

Klresmas Lest	Christmas List
1 Asshep	1. A spaceship
2 Bak RiGars	2. Buck Rogers
3 Flie awae agnFegr aF Suprman	3. Fly-away Action Figure of Superman
4 God Zliia	4. Godzilla
5 MeDm sis shognwers	5. Medium-sized Shogun Warriors

Their writing topics are those that they have enough background and interest in to be able to communicate.

A writing center is set up with supplies for children to use and choose those implements that best suit their purposes. Markers, pencils, crayons, tape, assorted kinds of paper, blank books, scissors, and staplers are readily available all year. A shelf has copies of stories on display that were written by children in previous classes. It is exciting to read a book written by a friend, and children are anxious to try writing one themselves. Their proficiency increases gradually as they become young authors.

I read to my students daily from factual sources as well as literature. Several treasured books contain notes and autographs from authors that I have heard speak. As I relate how these professional authors use real-life happenings and put them into story form, writing is de-mystified.

As children deal with their own real experiences, they need to have many books available to read and enjoy themselves. Over 2,000 books are found in the Reading Corner in my classroom. They give children the opportunity to discover how many different authors write. If writing is to flourish, the entire classroom must be a print-filled environment.

Guidelines for Teachers

In the classroom where children write, two principles must be considered: Writers proceed at different rates. Writers make errors.

How a teacher reacts to these facts will have an effect on what children write. To expect all children to do the same assignment or to create a perfect first draft places an artificial constraint on the learner.

In any classroom there are a variety of learners who bring varied experiences and abilities with them. Developmental psychologists from the Gesell Institute (1955) stress that in any description of behavior characteristics of age levels, all children will not behave just the same; children give their own individual twists to these age sequences. Looking at two first-grade writers, Tagg wrote about 2,700 words in one year while Laurie wrote over 10,000. Tagg began with all capital letters while Laurie used lower case appropriately. Tagg used invented spellings while Laurie used conventional forms. Both were normal first-grade children. It was not appropriate to expect them to proceed at the same rates and be able to complete the same assignment. As language learners they were very different, yet both reflected a need to communicate. With open-ended activities, they did not become discouraged or convinced they could not write. Both had an opportunity for continued development and a chance to become effective writers.

As researchers look at writing, they note that children write differently than adults. These 'errors" are not made because of a lack of knowledge, but because of knowledge that grows while they are constructing language to make it their own. Marie Clay (1975) noted that the gross approximations children made later became refined; correctness was not a first stage but a later refinement of initial approximations. She discovered that one new insight could change a child's writing, even disorganize it. It is entirely possible that it may look as if a child has forgotten something previously known, but the child is actually reflecting new knowledge.

Charles Read (1975) found children to be consistent in their judgments of phonological relationships. Children use articulatory features to make spelling decisions that are different from those adults make. Several children have illustrated this principle in my classroom. As Tiffany writes to me, she often uses my name. She began by copying it from my mailbox as she wrote HI MISS MILZ on September 7. In October, she tried to write my name independently: I LIKE YOU MESS MELS. Since then, she has returned to using MISS MILZ, but she is able to write without first going to a printed source or asking someone else how to spell it. Rhea Paul's kindergarteners (1976) tackled each word they wrote as a new creation, and often came up with a different solution than they found before. Glenda Bissex (1979) noted that her son's spellings evolved through a whole series of changes.

Writing is complex as children deal not only with spellings, but with capital and lower case letters, manuscript and cursive writing, punctuation, sentence structure, the expression of meaning, and various forms all at the same time. All the researchers noted have observed a gradual move to conventional forms and found that error did not stay with a child as a bad habit.

Summing Up

Young writers are engaged in a process of language development. They are using their existing knowledge of language and their capacity as humans to develop it further. At every grade level, there is need to communicate and record thoughts. There is a message in any attempt to write. It is of value to the child that produced it, and it must be treated as valuable through the acceptance and encouragement of the recipient. As teachers, parents, and others respond in this way to children's writing efforts, children will become confident writers, like Jennifer. She was a second grader when she gave me this note on April 2, 1979. (See Figure 3.)

dear Miss Mils
at The end of The gear
Iam going To miss gou
Becous next gear I wont
Be hear in your class Room
But Still I will vesit gouand
Show gou some of my Books
and in The Summer Time
I will writ Letters. I wish
gou wolud Be my Techer
next gear gou help me Read
gou help me writ and gou
make me happy.
Love Jennifer

Figure 3. Sample of confident second-grade writing.

A Functional Writing Program for the Middle Grades

Joanne Yatvin
Crestwood School, Madison, Wisconsin

Although the problem of poor student writing has been with us for a long time, the solutions proposed have not changed much over the years. Essentially, there are two beliefs. One, which gained a brief ascendancy during the sixties, holds that children learn best through free, imaginative writing experiences on which adult standards of correctness are not imposed. The other, long popular and now once more ascendant, asserts that strict standards, coupled with systematic instruction in grammar, punctuation, and spelling are the keys to good writing. Perhaps because of these unbalanced approaches, many children have not responded well to writing instruction. Far fewer have become competent in this skill than their intelligence and abilities in other areas would lead us to expect.

Considering the spotty successes achieved through these two approaches, it seems strange that a functional approach—one that adopts the motivations and methods of people writing in the real world—has never attracted a strong following. Functionalism promises to succeed where other approaches have failed because it brings together creativity and correctness and provides relevant, timely teaching. It holds that students can learn to write well if they have real purposes for writing, follow realistic procedures, and receive instruction that meets their needs at the time of need. Though some teachers have developed their own techniques for teaching functionally, there are few complete programs anywhere, and this view of writing is conspicuously absent from textbooks. Thus, there is a need to turn the functionalist philosophy into a teaching program that can be used throughout the grades. This chapter reports the efforts of a small group of teachers to create and teach such a program at their grade level.

In 1975, four fourth and fifth grade teachers at Crestwood School in Madison, Wisconsin, dissatisfied with established practices, began to explore the possibility of a functional approach to their composition instruction. Their years of experience, professional reading, graduate coursework, and personal insights had already led them to try many innovative techniques, but now they were ready to plunge into a total program. Joined by their principal, they began to design their writing curriculum. Realizing that it was impossible to duplicate all the conditions of real world writing experience with children in the confines of the classroom, they decided to adhere to three basic principles of functionalism in student purposes and procedures and teacher methods, compromising with necessity in less vital matters.

Basic Principles of Functionalism

1. Purpose would govern all classroom writing. Not only would students have a real purpose for everything they wrote, but all formal, technical, and stylistic considerations would grow out of that purpose.
2. As far as possible, children would do the various kinds of writing people do in the real world and follow the same kinds of procedures.
3. Teaching would be a supportive process. Rather than concentrating efforts on instruction separate from writing or post-writing correction, teachers would provide assistance throughout the writing process.

In order to give themselves clear and concrete guidance for their day-to-day teaching, they broke down these principles further into teaching guidelines.

Teaching Guidelines for the First Principle

A. Every writing experience should begin with the identification of a purpose and an audience.
B. Purposes should emerge from classroom activities and interests but, if at times they come from an outside source, children should agree that they are worth writing for.
C. Once a purpose is identified, children and teacher should select the appropriate forms, styles, conventions, and mechanics for meeting it, adapting what they already know to the need and learning whatever new elements are necessary.

D. Instruction in spelling, usage, punctuation, and capitalization should be integrated into writing, not taught in isolation. If an item does not come up naturally in writing, perhaps it is not necessary for children of this age to learn it.

E. Since workbooks, worksheets, and drill exercises are not related to any purposes of real world writing, they should not be used in the classroom.

F. Completed written work should be judged by its effectiveness in serving its purpose and reaching its audience.

Teaching Guidelines for the Second Principle

A. The distinction between public and private writing and their attendant characteristics should be made. Public writing goes to a large and/or unfamiliar audience who will judge it at least partly on neatness and correctness; private writing is for one's self or one's intimates and is judged on communicative effectiveness alone.

B. Classroom writing tasks should reflect—although they cannot duplicate—the range of writing tasks that people do in the real world, from lists, to messages, to poetry.

C. Before writing, children need a time for thinking, planning, and oral exploration of a topic.

D. The writing process should cover sufficient time—preferably a period of several days—so that children can talk about, think about, revise, and recopy their work before calling it done.

E. Finished written work that is going to a public audience should be neat and correct, just as effective examples of public writing in the real world are.

F. Children should not be asked to tinker with prepared writing samples deliberately loaded with errors and confusing choices. Such exercises are not a part of real world writing.

G. Teachers should not write comments, corrections, or grades on completed papers for which they are not the audience. They may comment orally or on a separate sheet of paper, remembering that the time for improving this piece of writing is past.

Teaching Guidelines for the Third Principle

A. Classroom writing should be a group effort in which teachers and other students act as collaborators, editors, and critics all along the way.

B. Instruction before writing should include models or frames,[1] oral exploration of the topic, demonstration of proper use of mechanics likely to be needed, and the development of a plan for writing. The object of preparation is to make children feel they can handle the task.

C. At every step of the writing process, children should have full access to the people and materials that can help them, whether their needs are for information, words, spellings, or reactions to what they've written so far.

D. All pieces of public writing need a thorough editing phase which includes emotional reactions, substantive criticism, and technical assistance.

E. Since more than sixty years of educational research have failed to demonstrate that a knowledge of formal grammar helps people to write better, grammar instruction should not be a part of writing instruction.[2]

Because many things advocated in the guidelines were as yet unproved and some things prohibited were traditional staples of language arts teaching, it seemed wise to test the program empirically before making a final commitment to it. In two stages over two years, the writings of Crestwood School students were compared to those of students in two similar schools where more traditional writing programs were being taught. Because parents were skeptical about the lack of separate instruction in spelling, grammar, etc., these aspects of the program were tested first. The results showed that Crestwood students did just as well as their counterparts who had received separate, specific instruction. In the second stage, writing quality was tested, revealing that Crestwood students did substantially better than the others.[3] Reassured by these results, the teachers moved into the third year of their program intent upon extending and refining classroom

---

1. Terms will be explained later on.
2. See, for example, Richard Braddock, Richard Lloyd-Jones, and Lowell Schoer, *Research in Written Composition* (Urbana, Ill.: National Council of Teachers of English, 1963) and W. B. Elley, I. H. Barham, H. Lamb, and M. Wyllie, "The Role of Grammar in a Secondary School English Curriculum," *New Zealand Journal of Education Studies*, May 1975:26-42.
3. Joanne Yatvin, "A Meaning-Centered Writing Program." *Phi Delta Kappan* 60 (1960): 680-681.

practices. Although they did not change any of their principles or guidelines, there has always been much more involved in teaching than was explicitly stated in them, and, therefore, further explanation of the program is needed. Described below is the day-to-day operation of the Crestwood Writing Program as it existed in 1980.

Classroom Climate

More than most curricula, a functional writing program depends on a certain classroom climate to flourish. You can't convince children that doing things the way people do them in the real world is important in one area while denying it in others. The functional organization of our classrooms at all grade levels existed before the writing program and, to some extent, probably gave rise to it. But we have endeavored to extend that functionalism to the limits of our capacity as a public school in a city system and as responsible caretakers of children from fairly conservative families. For one thing, all our classrooms contain two grade levels well mixed, and by October few children can remember who is in one grade and who is in the other. This organization was instituted because we believe that having children of different ages work together is natural and a realistic accommodation to the problems of different speeds and abilities in one classroom. Not only does it provide "models" and "helpers" for the younger children, but it allows all children a wider range of acceptability in performance. In addition, it has the more subtle advantage of loosening grade level constraints on subject matter. Teachers are freer to use whatever textbooks seem right for their students regardless of the grade number stamped on their spines, and freer to toss them out altogether in favor of homegrown materials.

As far as possible, various subject areas are integrated, with the emphasis on learning through doing. Writing experiences flow easily and plentifully through this type of melange. Children are as likely to write an account of the behavior of a hibernating turtle, a book of verbal math problems, or a description of their community fifty years ago as a story for English. If a few collaborate on writing a play, it will be produced. If others set about writing poems, they will be illustrated, artistically inscribed, and "published" as a book.

In a functional climate, children feel that their classroom is part of the school community and also the surrounding adult community and that they are valued citizens of both. We have tried to facilitate this feeling by keeping people, things, and information flowing in all directions and by involving children in school and community projects. Our fourth and fifth graders make books for the school library and for children in lower grades; they help write the school rules; we talk to them as adults, ask their advice and cooperation, and try to respect their rights and feelings. They interact with our parents organization by sending proposals and representatives to meetings and by running booths at the annual school carnival. They get involved with the community by such projects as planting trees, cleaning up vacant lots, writing letters to newspapers, and inviting various adult groups to programs and parties at school. Maintaining the intensity and diversity of community activities is very difficult for teachers, who also have to teach subject matter, but our teachers believe that such activities pay off in learning.

Another aspect of classroom climate that is especially important to our writing program is clear, honest, concerned communication. In order for collaborative writing and editing to work, children have to learn how to give and take advice and criticism. And they have to learn to care about excellence in the other person's work as well as their own. The development of communication skills, which involve a number of intellectual, psychological, and linguistic factors, is not easy to identify in teaching or to describe. Some of it can be taught directly in the language arts program, but much more of it comes piecemeal, spread out over the entire curriculum and included in the way people in the classroom are expected to behave toward one another. Among the identifiable techniques our teachers use are (1) providing regular small group and partner activities, (2) encouraging talking as a part of working, (3) scheduling time for private teacher/student conversations, and (4) insisting that opinions voiced in public be supported by reasons.

Concomitant Teachings

Although our writing program is very tolerant of children's weaknesses during the writing process, it demands high technical standards on finished work. We believe that this dichotomy reflects the way things are in the real world: Writers may be as careless of conventions as they need to be while in the throes of creation, but once the product is ready to be delivered to its audience, they'd better get it into good shape. The attitudes and practices necessary for making written work publicly acceptable are not actually writing skills, but since they are a part of the functional view of writing, we teach them along with the program. One is the development of the concept of public discourse and its characteristics. Children learn that newspaper articles, library books, comic strips, and advertisements have a specific purpose and an intended audience. Often, they are asked to judge how well pieces they've read served their purposes and communicated with their audiences. They also observe that professionally published writing is correct, neat, and attractive and discuss the importance of such characteristics when a large, unknown audience is involved. Although it is not feasible for students to visit a newspaper to observe the editing and reproduction procedures to transform a reporter's story into a published article, this would be an excellent activity for any class that could arrange it.

The second is the technique of proofreading, which is introduced early in fourth grade and put into practice gradually rather than applied full scale right from the first. Not only must children learn how to read for errors, they must first know what the common errors are. Besides being demanding, proofreading is a slow and unexciting business. Children, we have found, will try to avoid it or do it superficially. Therefore, our teachers reteach techniques from time to time, insist upon their careful use, and spot-check papers that have undergone the process. We are not at all tolerant about substandard work that has gone public. Children as well as teachers want to know who was responsible for letting errors slip through.

The Writing Process

The process used for all formal writing lessons has four phases: exploring, composing, editing, and going public. The steps involved in each phase are described below, but their order is not inflexible, and whenever steps don't fit a particular task they can be omitted.

Exploring Phase

1. *The writing purpose is set.* Most of the time writing projects grow out of previous classroom activities and interests, becoming just the natural thing to write next. But still the teacher may have to be the one to identify a need or a purpose that children do not perceive. The teacher might say, for example, "If we want people to come to our hobby show next week, I think we'd better do some advertising." I will not

pretend that purposes are not often "engineered" by teachers who, although they need not worry about covering a specified list of topics, do have to consider that learning demands variety and increasing difficulty. At times a teacher might frankly say to the class, "I think it's time for us to try our hands at books for the kindergarten again."

2. *The appropriate form(s) and intended audience are identified.* Working as a group, children decide on the type(s) of writing they will do to meet their purpose. If, as above, they are writing to advertise a hobby show, they might make posters, write invitations, and compose a notice for the school newsletter. Since the first product would be read by younger children and the second and third by adults, they have to consider how these differences will affect the task.

3. *Models are studied.* Samples from books or other published sources are studied to see how the task has been done by others. Children may borrow from or adapt a model according to the level of their skills. For example, novices at invitation writing might feel most comfortable just inserting their own information in a sample invitation from a textbook. The more experienced writers might prefer to create something completely their own.

4. *Specific teaching of technical matters is done.* The teacher teaches the fundamentals of techniques, forms, and conventions likely to be needed in this task, such as the capitalization of important words in a poster.

5. *Content and organization are discussed.* Children talk about the task as a group, exchanging ideas and suggesting different approaches. Together, they make a general plan for completeness and order to be used as a guide for writing. At this time they also brainstorm words they might want to use, and the teacher writes them on the board so that spellings are always available.

6. *Five minutes of silent thinking time are mandated.* During this absolutely quiet time children are supposed to make a final decision on what they will write and to personalize the general plan for writing. They may, of course, have more time if they need it.

Composing Phase

1. *First drafts are written.* Children put their ideas down on

paper, changing and shaping them as they go. They spell and punctuate as they think best. They may ask another child or the teacher for brief help, but are discouraged from interrupting themselves or their classmates for so long a time that they forget what they were writing. For example, a child should not have to leave his seat and wait in line to use a dictionary. If individual dictionaries cannot be provided, children should be trained to take chances on words or leave spaces. Inaccuracies can always be remedied later.

2. *The teacher helps where needed.* Moving around the classroom, the teacher looks for children who are stalled and tries to get them going again—giving needed words or spellings or suggesting a way out of a dilemma. If invited, the teacher may look over a completed first draft and encourage the writer to seek more precise words and better ways of saying things.

3. *Papers are collected.* The teacher keeps first drafts a day or two to allow children to get some distance from their work. All the papers are read during this time to get an idea of how things are going and what the specific problems are, but the teacher puts no comments or corrections on them.

Editing Phase

1. *Models are re-examined.* Children look at the models again in light of their own writing experiences and discuss likenesses and differences.

2. *Teaching for common weaknesses is done.* Drawing from what appear to be the general problems—both technical and substantive—the teacher teaches those elements. For example, invitations may be incorrectly punctuated or posters may be above the reading level of the children they are intended for. At the same time, a few typical papers (without names) may be read aloud for children to get an idea of group strengths and weaknesses.

3. *Editing of all papers is done.* Using a variety of exchange systems, the children read each other's work for strengths and weaknesses and to correct any obvious errors. To the extent that they are able, "editors" help writers to achieve clearness, completeness, order, appropriateness, and precision. Realistically, however, most children of this age can do little more than tell the writer whether they understand the writing and like it. The teacher may work individually with students whose papers need a lot of revision.

4. *Revision is done.* On the basis of editing suggestions and their own impressions, children rework their papers.

5. *Proofreading is done.* Writers *and* partners read all papers for technical errors.

6. *Final copies are made.* Children put forth their best efforts to make correct, neat, and attractive final copies of their work.

Going Public Phase

1. *Papers are readied for distribution to their intended audiences.* This may mean making envelopes for letters, binding pages into a book, or decorating posters. It is a construction step rather than a writing step.

2. *Class members share their reactions to the finished products.* There is a public display and discussion.

3. *The teacher evaluates.* After reading them carefully, the teacher offers oral or written comments about each paper, emphasizing positive features and a personal reaction to the communication as a whole. Improvements are not suggested at this point, nor are comments written directly on any paper being sent on to another audience.

4. *Papers go to their intended audiences.*

Suggestions for Writing

Although specific topics come and go as the needs and interests of children change, the types of writing our students do have stayed fairly constant over four years. This is the result partly of "engineering" to ensure varied experiences, partly of our stable curriculum during this time, and partly of the fact that different groups of children have proved to be not so different after all. The types of writing tasks given here are not offered as a comprehensive or mandatory list, but as the viewpoint of one group of teachers. Other teachers may choose from them, of course, but they are better advised to use them as a seminal device for creating their own lists and as a comparison guide for looking at the types of writing their students now do. If they are not trying their hands at most of the types suggested, why not?

> *Personal narratives*—descriptions of real experiences, autobiographies, descriptions of future plans; many class books possible, such as "Our Happiest Birthdays"

Personal feelings—explorations of inner experiences, hopes, and imaginings; books (e.g., "Feelings on the First Day of School") and poetry possible

Fiction—fairy tales, fables, science fiction, jokes, future tales, short stories, fictional diaries of famous people, fictional historical journals, "eye-witness" accounts of historic events, "what if . . .?" stories

Journalism—news articles, human interest stories, feature articles, advice columns, quizzes, weather reports, interviews, editorials

Poetry—many different forms to express feelings, experiences, and perceptions

Reports—observation records for science, informational essays for social studies, questionnaires, surveys, reports of interviews, biographies

Communications—business letters, personal letters, invitations, thank-you notes, letters to editors and other public figures, telegrams, notes, messages, and memos (really personal communications would not go through editing or public phases)

Public notices—posters, ads for newspapers, handbills, commercials for radio and television

Books—various types of class anthologies, individual fiction, poetry, study books (e.g., math problems), concept books (e.g., holidays of the year)

Opinions—statements of position on current issues

Instructions—recipes, directions for constructions, directions for reaching a destination, "how-to-do-it" essays

Book jackets—story summaries plus biographical data about author

Greeting cards

Comic strips

Plays and skits

Captions for pictures

Song lyrics

Do not make the mistake of trying to read any sequence into this list. Although developmental sequence is necessary in a writing curriculum, it can not be provided externally. Outsiders—including the teacher until the students have become familiar—have no way of knowing in which direction children's interests will take them or how fast and how far. Then too, sequence often depends more on what a writer chooses to do with a task at different times than on differences inherent in tasks. So the teacher and the students must determine their own sequence in a functional writing program.

Still, we have some advice drawn from our own experiences to offer. In the beginning of the year and whenever a new type of writing is being introduced, it is best to start with short, prestructured tasks and then to move on to freer variations and interpretations within the same type. This practice enables students to build competence and confidence before striking out on their own. When moving among types, obvious differences in difficulty should be respected: let students try picture captions before autobiographies. But for the most part, there is really no point in worrying whether a poem is harder than a business letter or a report harder than a news article. If a teacher is forced to choose between regulating difficulty and what it makes sense to write next, sense must take precedence. If a task is truly functional for children, they will rise to the occasion.

Supportive Devices

When children fail at a writing task, it is usually because they don't understand what is expected of them. Despite the teacher's instructions and explanations, critical points remain unclear so they flounder about producing some disjointed sentences that please no one. Because various types of writing tasks are familiar to us as adults and teachers, we do not realize that many are absolutely new to children. And we do not see that often their important characteristics are not all that obvious. Our explanations fail first because they are incomplete (from the child's point of view) and second because they are ephemeral. By the time children need our good advice, it is gone from their memory. In order to overcome the problem, our teachers use one of two supportive devices: the model and the frame.

As a common fixture of writing programs, the model needs no description here. It is superior to the teacher's explanation because it contains everything writers need to know and it remains with them while they write. Using a model requires ability to deduce significant characteristics from the text and then to synthesize one's own text from them. This is no mean feat! (Still, it is easier than trying to apply principles from an explanation that you didn't understand and only half remember.) Our teachers assist students by supplying several models—ideally, ones written by children—so that characteristics become more obvious by repetition and better defined by variation. Teachers also assist students by working through most of the deductive process with their classes, and by allowing those children who need it to near-plagiarize a model. One of the great virtues of a model is that children can use it as much or as little as they need. One child says, "Oh, I see how it works," and tosses it aside. Another keeps it right up front the whole time while writing, substituting new words only in the thought and structure laid out by someone else.

A frame is a more supportive—yet more restrictive—device than a model and is used when a new type of writing is especially difficult or writers are especially weak. It is a skeletal structure of a writing, given to children to use as their own along with full instructions on how to flesh it out. (See Figures 4 and 5.) In its extreme, it sets the shape of the writing, delineates the kind of material that should go into it, orders the parts, and even specifies the sentence structure to be used. In using a frame, a writer doesn't have to deduce anything; he merely imitates and fills in. But after using a frame once or twice, most children have figured out the form well enough to move on to their own versions of it. Then, it becomes only a model. Most of the frames we use with our classes are fairly loose, allowing considerable freedom to the writer.

Can you hear the ___wind as it sings through the trees___ ?
Can you see the _____ ?
Can you smell the _____ ?
Can you taste the _____ ?
Can you touch the _____ ?
When you do, you will know the _____ .

To the child: Fill out the lines with the name of a natural object and its actions as you recive them through your senses. Any of the objects listed below will work, but objects that don't move, such as a mountain, will be harder to write about. Try to keep each line ending about seven syllables long. You may rhyme last words, if you wish. Actions need not be realistic: the wind doesn't really "sing," does it?

Objects: cloud, sun, mountain, rain, tree, storm, snow, ocean, and anything else you can think of.

Figure 4. Sample frame for a poem.

To the teacher: In conjunction with this frame, read *Alexander and the Terrible, Horrible, No Good, Very Bad Day* by Judith Viorst. It makes a humorous survey of the various things that can go wrong in a child's life and his reactions to them.

As soon as I woke up this morning and ___saw it was raining___ , I knew it was going to be a bad day. . . .

To the student: Using this beginning, describe three to five things that might go wrong in your day. They could be about school, friends, parents, brothers or sisters, the weather, your own behavior, or objects that won't work the way you want them to. In each case, tell how you would feel and make an unrealistic threat, such as "I'll run away and join the Navy." Repeat the threat after each thing that goes wrong. In the end, have one good thing happen that cancels out all the bad ones and take back your threat.

Figure 5. Sample frame for a story.

I must add that children should not be forced to use frames if they feel they can meet their purposes without them. Because our teachers offer frames only when they believe that models alone are not enough support, most children welcome them. Those who do not are free to proceed on their own.

There is hint enough of plagiarism in our use of models and frames to make one wonder if perhaps they are bad teaching practices. Yet, I think they are no more so than putting training wheels on a child's bicycle. Soon one child will ride; soon the other will write. In the meantime, we supply the support they need.

Purpose for Writing

Still missing from this description of our program are the purposes that impel children to write. We cannot, of course, supply them. Purposes must come out of the lives of children as they work and play together. Yet, some readers may be tempted to use our program minus purpose. It would be easy enough to excise our techniques and transplant them in classrooms where teachers pick the topics, children write to please teachers, good grades are the goal, and papers go into the trash basket. As far as we know, they may even work for a while in such circumstances, but ultimately, like all gimmicks, they will prove unreliable. Without purpose to motivate writing, lead to a form, discipline language, and provide reasons for editing, revising, and recopying, our program is no better than a hundred others gathering dust on teachers' shelves. With purpose to bring it to life, it may be a solid foundation for teaching writing.

Romance Precedes Precision: Recommended Classroom Teaching Practices

Marlene Caroselli
City School District, Rochester, New York

A half-century ago, Alfred North Whitehead, an eminent Harvard professor who lectured widely about education, observed that there are rhythms in education, periodic alternations in the patterns of mental growth. He characterized intellectual progress according to sequential stages: the stages of romance, of precision, and of generalization. Learning, he maintained, was simply a matter of putting in order the ferment, or cognitive chaos, that surrounds every individual. He decried educators who would foist isolated facts and unrelated tidbits of information upon the minds of children who had not yet acquired a schema or framework upon which to build their impressions of the world around them. This, he felt, was the surest way to stultify the desire to learn.

A harbinger of teaching/learning philosophies that would predominate educational arenas decades later, Whitehead exhorted educators to teach children according to their stages of mental development. Whitehead soundly rejected the notion that children should simply accumulate facts, asserting that unless such facts have already been shared with children in broad, general terms, then segmented bits of knowledge become artificial and meaningless.

On the other hand, the child who has been exposed to the romance of language, for example, will subsequently be more receptive to the precision required by the study of language. Such a child will also reach the generalization stage much more readily than the child who has not undergone such a pattern of learning.

The teaching practices contained in this chapter illustrate Whitehead's basic premise—that children must be guided into developing a love of language before they are asked to acquire the precise knowledge of rules of language. Before requiring young people to become masters of the craft of writing, we must instill within them a desire toward mastery. If children are fascinated by *our* fascination with language, they cannot help but be captivated by the wonder of words. This wonder invariably leads to a desire to perfect expression, to use language with precision, to become a connoisseur.

Approximating Whitehead's stages of mental development, the practices that follow have been grouped according to grade levels. The section dealing with activities for the primary grades reflects the "romantic" approach; it describes methods of developing interest in language. In the activities for the intermediate grades, the reader will encounter ideas for helping children acquire precision in the use of language. And in the section for the junior high school grades, teaching practices that will assist students to generalize and to make applications of their knowledge are delineated.

Primary Grades

First-grade students at the Aloha Park Elementary School in Beaverton, Oregon, make their own books based on the reading of a story by their teacher, Barbara M. Getty. After Ms. Getty's students have heard the story, they cut and paste a picture to indicate their favorite part of the story. Once the picture is glued to a sheet of construction paper, the children write their own stories about the cut-and-paste picture.

Sixth graders are invited to join the class during the writing period to help the first graders with spelling or other writing problems. In some cases, Ms. Getty writes the story as the child dictates it. Once the stories are completed, the children staple their own stories to their pictures.

At the end of the day, the children form a circle on the rug. Some children read their own stories and present their pictures. When requested to do so, the teacher reads some of the stories. The next morning, as children enter the classroom, they select their own pictures and attached stories and tack them on the cork strip in the corridor for the entire building to enjoy.

"If anyone had told me two or three years ago that first grade children could write and read their own stories during the first quarter of any school year, without benefit of many months of formal reading instruction, I would have considered the idea ridiculous!" writes Helen Reynolds of the Atkinson Academy in Atkinson, New Hampshire. Like Ms. Getty, she has discovered that young children sufficiently awakened to the romance of using words can produce pieces of writing which, in time, become more and more precise. The process that she describes reflects Donald Graves' comments cited in the first chapter of the monograph regarding teachers' estimation of what children can and should do during the first week of school:

On the very first day of school, I begin by giving each child a large piece of newsprint, crayons, and a pencil. I ask the children to "write" something to me. It can be anything that they wish. I do not specify, because I want to see what word "write" means to them and also what their capabilities are.

As I circulate around the room, stopping to give words of encouragement or a smile to an apprehensive child, I can observe many things: a name scrawled across the whole paper; large sized numbers; various upper and lower case letters of the alphabet, some reversed and/or upside down; scribbles; criss-crossed lines; bright colors; stilted pictures and action pictures; and some words like *dog, cat,* and *love.* Each paper shows me many levels of maturity, development, and knowledge and can be used at a later time to group children of similar ability. Some children are "all done" in less than five minutes, while others show a longer attention span. As each child finishes, I encourage that the paper be shared with me and I jot down what the child tells me. Then I stamp the day's date on it and we tack it up on our bulletin board, which has been divided to give each child a place where future writings will be displayed.

Drawing is writing to young children; it is also talking out a story and sharing it with someone. Their drawings and the knowledge of six to ten consonants are enough to help children get the flow of writing. As their knowledge of initial and final consonants, blends, and vowels begins to turn into words, words into phrases, and phrases into complete thoughts, real stories evolve. Each day there is a time for all to write and each piece is dated, shared, and then added to their collections.

The stages of growth and improvement are very evident to anyone who reads the child's earliest to latest writings. As the teacher, I show that I am affected by what the child has to offer and this in turn gives the child added incentive to continue writing.

Most children do not realize their own potential. We have never before asked them to write so early. Now they just conclude that they *can* do it . . . and do!

John Gaydos of the Atkinson Academy in Atkinson, New Hampshire, employs sensing of an audience for the writing to lure the recalcitrant writer to the romance of writing. Mr. Gaydos depicts the process in his own words:

With a second grader, Mark, I was stymied because the rest of the class seemed to be flowing and he was still clogged up. Mark would consistently explain his lack of writing by saying that he didn't know how to spell. Mark's school background had consisted of considerable prewriting and writing activities, but he was out of synch with his peers. The elements of a normal sequence that beginning writers go through—prewriting (drawing, rehearsing, storytelling), invented spelling (experimenting with a minimal number of phonic elements to write stable recognizable words), and authorship (recognition and concern with audiences) —were all bearing on Mark with equal force and negatively affecting his ability to communicate a story in any form. In typical second grade fashion, he was obviously discovering the audience. He would anxiously begin his turn in a group sharing session with a lot of enthusiasm, but would quickly stop. Mark wanted the audience badly, but he didn't have a story to share, only beginnings.

In individual conferences I would press for getting the written word on paper but what I really needed to work on was content; the audience would be with him if he could tell a good story. I had mistakenly made a rule that said in order to share with the whole group, one had to have some written material started. Revoking the rule freed Mark to work solely on the content; now he could work on getting to his audience with a whole story.

Mark started his next story, "The Flood," with the understanding that when he had finished just the pictures he could share it with the whole group. Mark worked quickly at first, then slowed, but two individual conferences and one small group conference later, Mark had finished his illustrations. After hearing Mark tell his story, the group reacted very positively, some not believing Mark had actually done it. The more important fact was that Mark really knew he had captured an audience solely because of his story rather than because of his more typical aberrant behaviors.

Once Mark had, on his own, made a concrete connection to a sound/symbol relationship, he was ready to make an initial mental commitment to writing. Phonetically he had always had enough elements to record all he wanted to say, but it was his making a concrete tie between his phonics skills and the whole communication process that made Mark begin to flow. Mark's next story was written first and then illustrated.

I had grown, too. I had been seeking only written products and making pat assumptions about second graders' writing abilities rather than paying attention to individuals and the whole process of communicating.

Mary Ellen Giacobbe of the Atkinson Academy in Atkinson, New Hampshire, utilizes writing conferences in her first grade writing program. She stresses pupils' competencies as she confers with them. By giving positive attention to the skills children have acquired, she is able to enhance their positive feelings about writing and about themselves:

> During a writing conference, the child reads the piece. I retell the story giving the writer the opportunity to say, "Yes, that's the way it is," or "No, you don't understand." I do not interfere by giving my ideas. Instead, I ask questions that enable the writer to rethink the content. "What do you think about your story? What is the best part? Why? Are there any other details that you can add? What are you going to do next with this piece of writing?" The writer then has the choice to rewrite or not to rewrite.
>
> Once the content is the way the writer wants it to be, I focus on reading and mechanical skills. I mention all the things that the child was able to do. Then I choose one skill to work on. I record what happened during the conference in the writer's journal, as in this example:
>
> *December 15*
> Amy read *The Chipmunk*. She used *bl* and *ch*. She put a period at the end of each sentence. She remembered *ing* and used it in the word coming. We talked about *sh*. She wrote show, shop, ship and fish.
>
> On the first page of the journal is a growing list of skills that the writer has acquired. It might look like this:
>
> *Things Amy Can Do:*
> 1. Amy can put her name of the piece of writing.
> 2. Amy can put the date on the piece of writing.
> 3. Amy can put a period at the end of each sentence.
> 4. Amy can put *s* at the end of a word to mean more than one.
>
> Because Amy used *ing* correctly, I would add this to her list. On future pieces of writing, Amy is responsible for paying special attention to the skills on her list. When Amy has a conference, I help her by saying, "Check numbers 2 and 4 in your journal and then reread what you have written and make any necessary corrections."
> I am not responsible for content or red penciling all the errors. The child is given the opportunity to take increasing responsibility for individual writing and learning.

Andrea Giuffre of School #4 in Rochester, New York, uses writing to determine if children have understood certain historic concepts and facts. Andrea believes that if a student can take the facts, assume the role of an individual who lived in a given historical era, and tell a story set in that era, then the child has demonstrated a command of the historical concepts. Ms. Giuffre describes the procedure this way:

To associate with the reversal of time, students are asked to step into an imaginery time machine and to turn back the dials of time. At the chalkboard, periods of years are subtracted from the present year until the destination in time is reached. During this time, a class discussion describing the various signs of the times is held. As students enter the desired era, they note what has been left behind in modern lives and discuss what they will have to do without in the era they are entering. For example, if they are about to land on Plymouth Rock, they comment on the fact that no motel reservations have been made and that there is no restaurant at which to dine, nor a disco for entertainment.

Once the stage has been set, the children are divided into committees of four. To encourage reasoning and problem-solving, the children are asked to investigate facts, speculate, find solutions, and make alternative decisions about the historical destination to which they will travel. The children work in committees of four during this time. A child designated as recorder takes notes for the group and has the responsibility of guiding the course of the discussion. As children make decisions about their journey, the recorder writes down what the group has decided; however, all members of the group are expected to check spelling and to be certain that facts and reasoning are accurate. The teacher circulates among the groups and offers assistance when necessary. After fifteen or twenty minutes of group discussion, the recorders share the group's plans. The plans are then questioned, compared, contrasted, and summarized.

Having recreated an historical experience for themselves through a group process, the children are ready to assume individual identities as historical figures and to tell their stories by using the first person and either the past or the present tense. The following piece of writing was produced by a third-grade student in conjunction with a unit on the War of Independence.

> One day I was drinking a potion and I disappeared. I was in the future and then I fell on the ground and I was in 1776. I was in the Revolutionary War. George Washington thought I was a soldier. He said, "Get your gun!" I got the gun and started shooting.
> We won the war. And I said, "I want to go home." then I disappeared and went home.
> My mother said, "Robert, where have you been?" I said, "Oh, I was just out fighting."

Caren Barzelay Stelson, a third grade teacher in the Wellesley (Massachusetts) Public Schools, uses children's writing as a source for spelling study lists. Ms. Stelson explains the process:

> On Monday afternoon the children are handed back their daily writing folders from the previous week. They choose ten circled words from their story for their week's spelling list. They choose

willingly and reasonably. The resulting list of words is appropriate because the child has found them useful, but difficult to spell.

Once the words are selected, the children write them in their spelling list book, in their homework list, and in their writing dictionary. This dictionary is an alphabetized collection of the year's spelling words available for reference.

After the spelling lists are finished, the homework directions are explained. The homework is due on Friday and the children are responsible for completing it on time. The specific exercises vary each week, but each assignment is a mixture of practice and creativity. Students may be asked to write a story or poem, invent a spelling game to be played in school, or perhaps create a crossword puzzle or word hunt. Each exercise must incorporate those ten spelling words.

At home, the parents are asked to give a pre-test early in the week and a post-test at the end of the week. Parents check and sign the homework before it is returned to school. This motivates the children to seek out their parents for help and allows the parents to become more involved in their child's learning process.

On Friday morning, the homework is collected. The children share their projects with the class and positive comments are encouraged. In the afternoon, the children select partners, exchange spelling list books, and give each other their final spelling test. Each child says the word and gives a corresponding context sentence. The partners then correct each other's tests. As they check each word, they may learn new vocabulary which may enrich their future writing.

This year my spelling program makes sense. The children are struggling to write and in the process have understood the need to spell.

Intermediate Grades

Children's natural affinity for rhyme is employed by Mrs. Arls Stamm of the Crestwood School in Madison, Wisconsin. Stressing writing for a purpose and specific audience, Mrs. Stamm attempts to have the work of her fourth and fifth graders displayed in several different places. Prewriting, composing, editing, and publication are the four steps followed in all assignments. Models are used to introduce forms and to help set standards of quality. The following activity, based on Sandol Stoddard's *From Ambledee to Zumbledee*, provides an opportunity for children to explore language through the precision in the four steps involved in the composing process:

After having read lines of poetry aloud in order to feel the rhythm of the poem, the children discuss how beats need to be the same in each line so the poem "sounds right." The class then decides to make an alphabet book about imaginary insects that will be placed in the school library. Each student is responsible for a four-line poem with a rhyming pattern of AABB; each student is assigned a certain letter of the alphabet and selects an original but pronounceable name for an insect beginning with this letter.

Before actually writing, the children jot down several descriptions and actions they might want to include. It is pointed out that the poems are actually mini-stories and that—while a story might be wild and crazy—each line should lead to a logical conclusion. The first line includes the bug's name and tells something about the appearance, personality, or habitat. Lists of rhyming words are compiled to assist students with subsequent lines.

Following the composing stage, peer evaluation is used for the editing stage. Children share their work with each other and receive suggestions for improvement from each other. They also submit names for titles which are later voted upon.

The poems are typed and children draw their illustrations. After the books have been "printed," each child receives two copies. The library is given a copy of "A Bugwalk through the Alphabet," and the remaining copies are sold. The beginning of the Bugwalk follows:

A is for Affenter

An affenter is found down near the sea;
He gurgles with his mouth and drinks with his knee.
When he drinks cherry soda, his leg is in the glass,
And *he* still thinks he's got a lot of class.

In an effort to encourage student writers to become more precise in their written expression, Patricia Howard of the Atkinson Academy in Atkinson, New Hampshire, involves her students in sharing and critiquing each other's work:

> In writing, as in other disciplines, children can learn as well from their peers as from a teacher. I have set aside a large carpeted area in my fifth-grade classroom for what we have come to call "share." It is here that a child reads his or her story or draft and asks for comments. This special area removes the aura of the classroom setting, and becomes a place for the exchange of ideas.
>
> The first time my class came to "share," they were apprehensive about reading their stories. As we sat in a large circle on the rug, I explained the purpose of sharing and we discussed some rules. We would sit quietly with our papers on the floor, listen only to the person reading, raise our hands, etc. Only a few children were willing to read, but I knew this was only the

beginning. I called on someone who could accept criticism and we began our learning through sharing.

Steve read his piece and I raised my hand. "I loved the part when you said your stomach felt like a drum." Steve chose a friend to comment. "That's a super story!" Other positive comments followed. Then came a question about the sequence of events. Suddenly several hands went up, each child offering a suggestion to Steve. The class then realized the importance of revision in making their stories even better.

The children now insist on "share" for about twenty minutes after each writing period. I am able to sit back and wait for them to comment and question before interjecting my thoughts. So many of the pieces, however, offer such excellent learning experiences that I zero right in on them. "How did you feel when. . . ? Can you tell me that in your story? Doesn't your story really begin when. . . ?" These are but a few model questions I ask during our conferencing "share." Very soon the children ask them of not only the writer, but of themselves as they are writing.

Teaching writing through conference type sharing is easy since the children don't suspect that I am "teaching." It's fun for them and they take the information and incorporate it in their stories without even realizing that we have just had a lesson in writing.

Whitehead asserts that from the age of eleven on, children are most receptive to seeking and acquiring a precise knowledge of language. The study of literature, composing, and the elements of language should receive focus during this period of precision when a child is developing skills to perfect writing and reading. Critical thinking and listening skills should also be stressed during this period.

Sylvia Levinson, who reads stories over a period of weeks to her fifth graders at the Burtsfield Elementary School in West Lafayette, Indiana, helps her students to acquire proficiency in each of these skill areas with assignments such as this one, based on Scott O'Dell's *The Island of the Blue Dolphins:*

The book was read to the class by the teacher over a period of six weeks. Vocabulary was studied and discussions were held in conjunction with the reading. Creative and critical thinking and listening skills were stressed. Five movies depicting the sea and animal life typical of the book's setting were shown. The assignment, made as the book was nearly finished, was to write a complete description of one of the many exciting adventures and difficult problems Karana experiences. Suggested topics included "A Meeting with Strangers," "Enemy Turned Friend," "Attacked by Wild Dogs," "Caught in the Earthquake," "Alone and Afraid," "Rescued."

Each story was evuluted with a positive comment. Suggestions for improvements were made in writing and explained in conference. Compositions were graded with "√" "√+" or "√++." Stories were read to the class, and additional suggestions and reactions were given to the student writers. Later, the overhead projector was used to show and correct common grammatical errors. Each child was encouraged, although not required, to revise the product and resubmit it.

Note the careful choice of words in the following piece of student writing which resulted from this assignment.

> The wild dogs have been my enemy ever since they killed my brother Ramo. I started to make some spears and a bow and arrow. After I finished them, I set out with two spears and my bow and arrow to find the pack of wild dogs. When I did, the pack spread out, except the leader. He just stood there, unafraid, his big yellow eyes staring at me. Then I shot my arrow. It struck him in the chest. He took one step and fell. Taking my weapons, I climbed off the ledge and went to the place where the leader had fallen. I went into their lair. Beside a half-eaten carcass of a fox lay a black dog and four pups. I came out of the cave. I started for my house. Along the path I found the leader, lying there, very still. I went over to him and pulled the arrow out. He whined, and then was quiet. I wasn't sure if he was dead. Suddenly, I hoped the wound wouldn't kill him.

To encourage students to select exact words for their imaginative writing, Ava Marie Smith asks her class of fifth graders at the South Frederick Elementary School in Frederick, Maryland, to assume the persona of a given object. The practice follows:

The teacher brought a pair of roller skates into the classroom and told the children that their writing would have something to do with the skates. The class discussed what the skates were, what they were used for, who had them, and where they could be found. The skates were then passed around and children talked about their compositions. The children were told that they were to actually "become" the roller skates.

They discussed among themselves how they would approach the topic. Ideas and enthusiasms were exchanged. Students were then given time to write and edit their stories. The following day, they were given time to discuss their stories, write them over, and illustrate them.

As the children wrote, the teacher circulated around the room and listened to their ideas. The teacher, however, did not point out mechanical errors until the children were in the editing or revising stage.

To assist teachers to make writing a natural part of the total instructional day, Frederick Wille of the East Aurora Union Free School District, New York, has suggested three steps for enriching the writing program in the elementary classroom.

There are vast and diverse opportunities for children to write. In order for the elementary classroom teacher to become more aware or sensitive to the various possibilities that exist, these steps may provide a suitable starting point to stretch the writing process in the elementary classroom.

1. Review lesson plans for a given instructional day. By using some sort of code, indicate which activities involve writing. Follow the same procedure by reviewing previous plans of at least one week. Determine if there are any patterns emerging. This task will enable the teacher to identify some areas of the curriculum (other than language arts) in which writing is done with some degree of frequency.

2. The second phase of this awareness-building is to brainstorm all the incidental, informal occasions where writing takes place. Since these activities typically involve fewer constraints, writing is accomplished in a more relaxed atmosphere. Therefore, these writing experiences are generally weighted with less importance than other writings. These activities can serve as excellent points of departure for improving writing and for giving writing a higher place of importance. The teacher now possesses two documents of information pertaining to the children's writing. These will serve as valuable tools in furthering children's writing in the classroom.

3. The third piece of information that the teacher needs to acquire comes from the children. Draw up a simple form—a questionnaire that asks the children to list the types of writing they do that is unrelated to school. On this form you would also need to ask the approximate frequency for each type of writing. In addition, you may want to ascertain their feelings about these writing acts. Some sort of values continuum could yield this information very quickly and easily.

Upper and Junior High School Grades

The junior high school student, according to Whitehead, is completing the stage of precision and preparing to enter the stage of generalization, in which students respond well to the ideas contained in literature. Students at this age should be given the opportunity to apply what they read to other situations.

Questions pertaining to their reading are less literal, and more interpretive in nature. Students are better able to handle more abstract thought processes and to evaluate the characters and situations about which they have read.

In her work with children who are reading several years below grade level, Germaine Froehlich of Jefferson Junior/Senior High School in Rochester, New York, has students apply what they have read to a writing task. Using the black folktale "How the Snake Got Its Rattles" by Julius Lester (recorded by Ossie Davis), Mrs. Froehlich introduced a unit on folktales and legends by having the students read the stories silently while listening to the recording.

After a discussion of the story and of the elements such as hyperbole which are integral parts of the tall tale, the students wrote tales of their own, based on the Lester story. When the stories had been written and illustrated by the students, they were typed by the teacher. The mini-anthology was then dittoed and sent home to parents as a gift. Mrs. Froehlich, in sending home the stories to parents, encourages her students to write for others; in so doing, she is able to correlate reading proficiency with writing proficiency.

"How My Bird Got Its Beak"

> Once upon a time my bird Kojack did not have a beak, so he could not eat peanuts or sunflower seeds. All he could eat was soup. One day he got so sick of this situation that he prayed to the Lord to give him a beak so he could eat sunflower seeds and peanuts. My bird went to sleep that night.
>
> In the morning, he woke up and saw that he had a beak. When he said, "Polly wants a cracker," no one could hear him. He waited until we all woke up and then he repeated, "Polly wants a cracker." Then we saw the beak. My sister went to get a cracker, and he ate it. Ever since then he's been crunching away.

The following set of teaching practices has been submitted by Mary Anne Mount of the Columbia School in Decatur, Georgia. Ms. Mount, in an attempt to develop students' ability to generalize and to deal with interpretation and abstraction, has found that the following activities are ones to which students respond well.

1. As a prewriting activity, students act out being on a crowded bus—without a seat—with arms full of packages.

2. The class discusses sights which would be seen (cheerleaders returning from a game, sitting in the back of the bus), sounds which would be heard (babies crying, radio playing), and smells (the exhaust fumes of the bus, pungent after-shave lotion).

3. In a stream-of-consciousness fashion, students record thoughts which might be going through their heads. (Oh, my aching feet!" "Get off my toe, you creep!")
4. The sensory impressions, as well as the verbal expressions, are then woven into a descriptive or narrative piece of writing.

A second activity which Ms. Mount finds useful in strengthening students' ability to interpret involves music:

1. The teacher plays several different kinds of music.
2. As each selection is played, students jot down associations made from the music. These may be images, scenes, memories, characters, etc.
3. Students then select one of the lists of associations and develop it into a story or play.

Jeannie Baxter and Jane Burris, middle school teachers in Snellville, Georgia, utilize a writing process approach in their writing program. Each student in their classes keeps a "day book," or personal journal, and makes entries in it at least several days a week. Class periods begin with a ten minute quiet writing time during which students either make entries in their journals or work on separate pieces of writing that they are developing.

During the remainder of a class period devoted entirely to writing, teachers and students engage in a variety of activities. Prewriting discussions related to finding a topic and deciding what the writer may do with it are held to help writers who are ready to start on a new piece of work. Teachers and students confer with writers who are shaping or polishing a piece. Students who are preparing to write on a topic requiring research utilize the school library media center. A general air of purposeful work pervades the classroom during writing sessions.

Once every two weeks a class period is set aside for reading aloud of in-process or completed work to the class as a whole. Discussion of techniques employed for the first time in recent writing and of their effectiveness is sometimes also held during this oral "publishing" period.

Summary

The classroom teaching practices reviewed in this chapter reflect creativity and care that teachers throughout the country bring to the teaching of writing. The activities are designed to capture the joy with which children initially respond to language. Enamoured of expression, children will easily move from the romance of language to the precision of thought, as Whitehead predicts. And, having passed through these two stages of language development, children will then be ready to deal with generalization and abstraction as their cognitive skills are sharpened.

They will be ready, if initially captivated by the romance of language, to acquire subsequent mastery of precision and generalization. That romance indeed precedes precision is perhaps best captured in the words of a fifth grader from the Penfield, New York, school system:

"Wasting Time"
by Christopher Quigley

I always
  waste time.
  I sharpen
    my pencil for
    spelling,
      break it
        to get away from
        reading,
        go to the
          bathroom
          for
            math,
              drop things
              for science,
              but waste
              no time
                for poetry.

A District-Wide Plan for the Evaluation of Student Writing

Roger A. McCaig
Grosse Pointe Public School System, Grosse Pointe, Michigan

The inability of high school graduates to express themselves in writing with clarity and conviction is a national disgrace. Theme and variations about this view have been delivered from a number of different forums by university officials, employers, political figures, representatives of community and parent groups, editorial commentators, and self-appointed experts. The truth of the claimed inability of students to express themselves in writing and of the alleged decline in student achievement in writing in the last two decades involves many complex issues which have yet to be resolved. One reason for this is that no generally accepted system for evaluating writing exists to confirm or disprove any of these claims. No doubt exists, however, about the reality of the public perception about writing in the schools. State testing, the establishment of minimal competencies for promotion or graduation, the voucher plan, earned categorical aid, and performance contracts are examples of strategies recently adopted by federal and state agencies, citizens' lobbies, and local boards of education in an attempt to force schools to improve student learning in the basic skills, especially reading and writing.

The expectations of parents whose children attend the public schools in Grosse Pointe, Michigan, are certainly no lower than those of parents in other communities, and interest in the acquisition and development of the skills of written expression is as keen in Grosse Pointe as it is elsewhere. The fact that students in the Grosse Pointe Public School System actually do write extremely well may or may not be different from student achievement in other communities throughout Michigan and across the country. What may be different in Grosse Pointe is that local teachers and administrators have a tool that permits them to make definitive statements about local achievement in writing.

Data exist, for example, to warrant drawing these conclusions:

> By the end of the second grade, virtually all students, without
> any help whatsoever, can compose a completed series of ideas
> about a topic in impromptu written expression.
>
> By the end of the tenth grade, 40 percent of students can write
> well enough to earn an A or B in a typical first-year college
> English class, and another 25 percent are not far behind.[1]

Claims such as these are, of course, dependent upon the appropriateness of the evaluation criteria and the integrity of the evaluation system as a whole. School districts have been known to make extravagant claims of success based on criterion reports for student learning which has turned out to be trivial or even misconceived. Thoughtful readers, therefore, will suspend judgment pending a review of the criteria and of the entire evaluation model. The same thoughtful readers will also be aware that, in the absence of any national test of writing ability, local school districts can do no better than to invent their own criterion measures and to compare the results for one year with the results for the next year to see if achievement is declining, stable, or improving. Such local efforts should be welcomed and encouraged as a constructive way to exchange promising practices and as the only solution currently available to local school systems to resolve a crucially important educational problem.

The success of the writing program in Grosse Pointe is due to many factors typically described as essential characteristics of a quality educational program such as excellence in teaching, careful definition and description of an integrated curriculum, effective instructional materials, and a continuous program of in-service training. In addition to these conventional components, the program for teaching writing includes other features which, while not unique, are somewhat less typical. One such feature contributing to the success of the local program is that the curriculum for teaching writing was established and validated by an analysis of the natural activity and actual performance of children and youth. Another critical feature is that the program includes a systematic plan for the annual evaluation of student writing.

Every aspect of an educational program needs to work effectively as part of a coordinated, integrated whole. The scope of this chapter is limited to a description of the evaluation component,

---

1. Approximately 65 percent of high school graduates from Grosse Pointe enter four-year degree-granting institutions of higher learning.

not because it is the most important element in a comprehensive plan but because it tends to be the component most likely to be missing. This chapter, then, is a description of the basic features of the system for evaluating student writing currently in use in the Grosse Pointe Public School System.

Plan for the Annual Assessment of Student Writing

Each spring, as part of annual achievement testing, every student in grades one through ten is required to select a topic from a number of choices and to write an impromptu paper with no assistance of any kind. On another day during the testing period, the process is repeated with a different set of topics. No opportunity is provided to revise the papers except during the thirty-minute testing period for elementary students and the forty-five-minute period for secondary school students. The purpose of the test is to assess the present competence level of each student, not to grade a final examination. Since performance in written expression is known to be more variable than it is in some other areas of school learning, the two trials are scheduled in an attempt to obtain the most accurate possible measure of competence.

The better of the two papers for each student is selected by the teacher, usually in conference with the student, and is submitted for central judging. A team of judges, three for each grade level, is selected on the basis of a judging of actual papers with known ratings. The three-judge team for each grade level then receives intensive training in applying the evaluation criteria to student writing. In the actual judging, each paper is independently rated by two different judges on a scale ranging from a low of one to a high of seven. If the rating differs in these two readings, the paper receives a third reading from a different judge.

Ten teams, consisting of three judges each, are used to conduct the evaluation for the ten grade levels. The reliability of the judging process has proven excellent. The average reliability coefficient for the thirty judges, based upon the degree of match between each judge's ratings and the final ratings assigned to each paper, was found to be .75 in a comprehensive study conducted for the 1979 evaluation of student writing.[2]

---

2. Office of Research and Development, the Grosse Pointe Public School System. *The Reliability of the Judging of the Writing Test*, Research Report No. 12, June 1980.

The judging process is not at all like the judging which occurs in a writing contest. Its purpose is not to rate the papers in the same way a teacher grades a paper for a specific assignment. It is to make holistic judgments about the present competence of each writer from the evidence available in writing. The overall evaluation, best understood as a generalized statement about the competence of the student, is recorded on the student growth record along with other test results, is reported to parents, and is accumulated with other scores into totals for the review of teachers and administrators.

The choice of seven for the number of levels derives neither from mysticism nor from some unrevealed theory. It represents nothing more than the pragmatic outcome of trial and error with several possible rating systems. In field testing, inter-rater agreement fell off sharply with eight, nine, or ten levels, and since the ratings translate to highly specific statements about student competence which are used for many different purposes, accuracy is crucially important. Since each rating represents a cluster of specific competencies demonstrated in the paper, it serves as an overall statement about each student's present skill in writing. Unless one is prepared to argue that a student can write a good paper by random luck, the rating must stand as conclusive evidence of skills attained. By inference, the level attained may also be interpreted in terms of the higher order skills not demonstrated in either of the two writing samples taken during the testing period.

Although the Grosse Pointe evaluation model was only recently extended to grades nine and ten, an annual assessment of student achievement in written expression has been conducted in the elementary grades since 1975. The system is accepted as standard practice throughout the school district by students, parents, teachers, and administrators and has long since lost whatever controversial overtones or Hawthorne effect it ever had as an innovation. Teachers emphasize instruction in the skill areas contained in the evaluation model. In addition to skill lessons and practice exercises, students have regular experiences "putting it all together," mostly because frequent experience in actual, purposeful, meaningful composing is the only method teachers have found which actually helps students become good writers. Drilling on skills alone does not produce good writers any more than backboard practice produces good tennis players.

Content of the Evaluation Model

For examples of the evaluation criteria, see Figures 6, 7, and 8. The criteria for grades three through ten can be described in general terms because certain underlying views about communication theory and language learning are consistent throughout the model. Perhaps the most pervasive theme running through all ten

---

For grades one and two, the levels represent stages of development based entirely upon the child's ability to communicate meaning in writing. The ability to use the conventions of written expression (correct spelling, punctuation, capitalization, etc.) is not evaluated until grade three.

Level 1—Beginning writing: The writing does not contain at least three complete thoughts that can be readily understood and are about the same topic.

Level 2—Beginning writing: The child can organize some complete thoughts and express them in writing. Some passages may not readily be understood. The ideas tend to be restatements of the same thought or to be a "list of sentences" with only one word different in each sentence.

Level 3—Beginning writing: The child can express a number of related ideas about a topic so that each idea after the first says something else about the topic or tells what happens next. Taken as a whole, however, the topic does not have a sense of completeness.

Level 4—Competent writing: The child can compose a completed series of ideas which are readily understood. The writing, however, consists entirely of basic sentence patterns.

Level 5—Highly competent writing: The child can compose a completed series of ideas about a topic, some of which are expressed in non-basic sentence patterns or contain a connecting word to join two main ideas. The ideas, however, tend to be expressed one at a time in simple sentences. The writing does not contain sentences packed with information and ideas.

Level 6—Superior writing: The child can compose a completed series of ideas about a topic and can compose complicated sentences, each with enough content to have been expressed in three or four simple sentences. The writing, however, does not contain insights or creativity.

Level 7—Superior writing: The child can compose a completed series of ideas about a topic with some complicated sentences and can compose with insight or creativity.

Figure 6. Evaluation criteria for levels of writing in grades one and two.

Level 1—Not competent: The writing does not contain an understandable message. It either contains passages that cannot be readily understood or contains an insufficient number of related thoughts to comprise a message.

Level 2—Not competent: The student can express a message that can be readily understood although the writing contains numerous deficiencies in wording, spelling, punctuation, or capitalization, judged by standards appropriate for the grade.

Level 3—Marginally competent: The student can express a message that can be readily understood and does not contain numerous gross deficiencies in wording, spelling, punctuation, and capitalization. The writing, however, is not competent in at least one of the following skills:

Completeness of content   Use of several non-basic sentence patterns
Sentence sense   Use of connecting words to join sentences
Spelling   Some use of subordination
Punctuation and capitalization

Level 4—Competent: The student can compose a completed series of ideas about a topic with the basic skills listed above at a level appropriate for the grade. The writing does not, however, demonstrate the use of good vocabulary, good sentence structure, a controlling idea, and some interpretation.

Level 5—Highly competent: The student can compose a completed series of ideas about a topic with basic skills at a level appropriate for the grade and with good vocabulary, good sentence structure, a controlling idea, and some interpretation. The writing does not, however, contain passages of superior writing with characteristics such as insight, creativity, or vitality of expression.

Level 6—Superior: The student can compose a completed series of ideas about a topic with excellent basic skills appropriate for the grade, with good vocabulary and sentence structure, with a controlling idea, and with a passage of superior writing. Superior writing contains characteristics such as insight, creativity, or vitality of expression.

Level 7—Superior: The student can compose a completed series of ideas about a topic with excellent basic skills appropriate for the grade, with good vocabulary and sentence structure, with a controlling idea, and with a sustained excellence of expression. The student can compose with insight, creativity, or vitality and richness of expression.

Figure 7. Evaluation criteria for levels of writing in grade six.

Level 1—Not competent: Content is inadequate for the topic selected, or deficiencies in the conventions of written expression are so gross that they interfere with communication.

Level 2—Not competent: The student can express a message that can be readily understood, contains adequate content for the selected topic, and demonstrates at least marginal command of sentence sense. The writing, however, is grossly deficient in one or more of these skills, judged by the standards appropriate for high school: spelling, usage, and punctuation and capitalization.

Level 3—Marginally competent: The student can compose a completed series of ideas about a topic with a minimum of gross deficiencies in spelling, usage, or punctuation, judged by standards appropriate for high school. The writing, however, does not contain at least one competent paragraph or is not competent in one or more of the following skills, judged by standards appropriate for high school: sentence sense, spelling, usage, and punctuation and capitalization.

Level 4—Competent: The student can compose a completed series of ideas about a topic with basic skills at a level appropriate for high school and with at least one competent paragraph. The writing, however, does not demonstrate all of the characteristics of highly competent writing:

Good overall organization   Good sentence structure

Competent paragraphing   Good vocabulary

Regular use of transitions   Appropriate use of subordination

Interpretive meaning (as opposed to literal writing)

Level 5—Highly competent: The student can compose a completed series of ideas about a topic with basic skills at a level appropriate for high school and with the characteristics of highly competent writing listed above. The writing does not, however, demonstrate thesis development and does not contain critical or creative thinking.

Level 6—Superior: The student can compose a completed series of ideas about a topic with excellent basic skills, with the characteristics of highly competent writing, with adequate thesis development, and with at least one passage demonstrating critical or creative thinking. The passage of superior writing, however, tends to be an isolated example.

Level 7—Superior: The student can compose a completed series of ideas about a topic with excellent basic skills, with critical or creative thinking, and with a sustained vitality and richness of expression.

Figure 8. Evaluation criteria for levels of writing in grades nine and ten.

grades is a reflection of a definition of writing implicit in this evaluation system. If there is a *basic* skill in the model, it is that the writing must communicate a clear message. Thus, this statement occurs as a descriptor of competence in written expression at every grade level: The student can compose a completed series of ideas about a topic which can be readily understood. . . .

Beginning in the third grade, Level 4 represents the attainment of locally defined grade level skills. The criteria for Level 4 always embody the statement about composing "a completed series of ideas" and then continue with standards for certain secondary basic skills such as spelling, sentence sense, punctuation, capitalization, and paragraphing depending upon the grade level described. Level 3 always means that the student can "compose a completed series of ideas" but has not demonstrated competence in one or more of the grade level skills. Level 2 is an indication of gross deficiencies in using language, and Level 1 is best viewed as pre-writing or nonwriting. On the high side of competence, Level 5 signifies mastery of all the basic skills set forth for a grade level plus certain other higher order skills for the grade such as vocabulary and sentence structure. Level 6 indicates evidence of interpretive or creative thinking, and Level 7 signifies a sustained richness and vitality of expression. The levels are additive in the sense that each level embodies all the abilities of all the lower levels and demonstrates, in addition, the higher skills defined for that level. Below is a generalized ladder-type description of the model:

Level 1—Not an understandable, completed message.
Level 2—An understandable message but grossly deficient in language skills.
Level 3—Not competent in one or more grade level skills.
Level 4—Competent for the grade level.
Level 5—Demonstrates higher order skills such as interpretation, vocabulary, and sentence structure.
Level 6—Exhibits interpretive or creative thinking.
Level 7—Exhibits sustained excellence of expression.

Special Consideration for the Primary Grades

The evaluation model for grades one and two differs in that it is developmental rather than skill-based. It is developmental in the sense that the levels correspond to key stages of growth and that virtually every student will progress through the stages at some time, although perhaps not in grade one or two. Classroom experience with the model has confirmed this hierarchy of levels in the primary grades for the great majority of children. It serves as a guide to help teachers recognize stages of growth and look forward to the next levels of development. It works as a sort of "A-ha!" system that brings daily rewards to teachers as they observe their young writers move up the ladder from September to June. The ladder concept works as long as a teacher recognizes that vaulting is not only possible but common. A student never demonstrates the criteria for Level 4 before attaining Level 3, but a student can vault directly from Level 2 to Level 4 without ever exhibiting the characteristics of Level 3.

The evaluation model for grades one and two differs in another way from the model for all the other grades. The conventions of written expression usually referred to as skills "don't count" until the third grade. The result is that the evaluation system for grades one and two is entirely meaning-based instead of being a combination of meaning and skills as in the higher grades.

The decision not to count skills in grades one and two created certain problems of definition in describing the evaluation criteria. The concept of sentence, for example, is an essential aspect of the evaluation model since the validation research discovered important differences in the ability of children to use constructions other than main clauses beginning with a noun phrase functioning as the subject and to use embedding techniques. Research has clearly demonstrated that kindergartners in their oral language use virtually all of the syntactic constructions used by older children, and local experience has shown that most children in grades one and two will attempt to use their full "inner language" in writing if encouraged to do so. The problem for the researcher is that children will attempt to express themselves in complex structures long before they transcribe all the function words, affix syntactic morphemes, and signal sentence boundaries with conventional punctuation and capitalization. This is a problem, it should be noted, only for the researcher, not for the child unless one chooses to make it a problem for children by requiring conventional orthography in the early stages of writing. Children literally can and should write complicated "sentences" before they ever learn what a sentence is.

The solution to this apparent dilemma was to invent a method of segmenting the writing of young children referred to as the *meaning unit*. A meaning unit is the idea thought to have been in the mind of the child during the process of composing. Each "sentence" (or meaning unit) composed by children in grades one and two, then, is a transformation of the graphic representations into the conventional sentence the child meant to express but may not have because of lack of experience and familiarity with written expression. This transformation is essential to the evaluation process because writing that contains *no* non-basic structures is considered developmentally lower than writing that does.

Development of the Evaluation Model

The evaluation model was not developed and validated by traditional techniques. The source for the evaluation criteria was not defined as the content of five of the eight most commonly used English textbooks, a procedure often used in validating the content of standardized tests. And it was not the opinion of a group of experts sitting around a big table deciding what student writing ought to be like. The data base for the development of the model was the actual writing of students. This decision about the process for developing the model is probably the primary reason for the remarkable applicability of the criteria as a way of looking at student writing and the even more remarkable improvement of student writing in the Grosse Pointe schools. The model works for instruction as well as evaluation because it is based upon the reality of what students actually can do, not a conception of what adults think students ought to be able to do.

The source for the data base was a collection of fifty to one hundred samples of impromptu student writing on each grade level. A committee of superior teachers for each grade level was assigned the task of reaching consensus judgments about the relative quality of each paper in the sample. Once the papers had been sorted and grouped into levels, the committee attempted to define the characteristics of the papers in each level and the differences between the levels. The definitions and descriptions developed by the committee were taken as hypothesized evaluation criteria. These trial criteria were then confirmed or negated by an actual analysis of the writing behavior in the papers. It is important to note that the collective, carefully considered impressions of the teachers serving on the committee often turned out to be wrong when tested against data derived from an analysis of the papers. Judgments, both positive and negative, about characteristics in one dimension of performance apparently tended to influence judgments about other characteristics. If the model had been developed solely from the opinions of specialists or even from the opinions of specialists attempting to describe actual student writing, the evaluation model would have turned out "wrong," judged in terms of the reality of learner behavior as opposed to the reality of teacher opinion.

The hypothesized criteria were then redefined, juggled, and manipulated until they satisfactorily accounted for the consensus ratings assigned by the judging team. The outcome of the entire inquiry was a simulated reconstruction of the intuitive responses of teachers to student writing, or at least, a hypothesized explanation of why the teachers rated the papers the way they did.

Treatment of Errors in the Evaluation System

The process of developing the system required a resolution of several issues essential to the content of the evaluation model. One crucially important issue for teachers as well as students is how to deal with "errors." Some evaluation systems count errors and derive some sort of score based upon the ratio of errors to total words or sentences written. This scoring method was rejected in the development of the model on the grounds that error behavior is typical of all learners, including adults, in the early stages of acquiring a new skill. Errors, in an important sense, can sometimes be regarded as signals that new learning is taking place, that the learner, having mastered some lower level skill, is attempting to extend known behavior into new environments or to explore totally new behavior. Since the model was designed to support and encourage student learning and good teaching, not just to rate writing, it had to be constructed in a way to distinguish between "good errors" and "bad errors" for each grade level. Otherwise, the evaluation system would force teachers to pressure students to write safely, rehearsing what they have already mastered, rather than to encourage students to reach out and try—even if the attempt is not fully successful.

This principle of learning is an intrinsic part of the evaluation system for every grade. In the elementary grades, for instance, the readers do not make their judgment about a student's command of sentence sense by examining dialogue or complicated sentences. Omission of an end stop in dialogue is ignored because of the special problems involved in the transcription and punctuation of oral language. A participial phrase standing as a sentence is treated as evidence of advanced sentence structure, not as a sentence error. A reasonable misspelling of a non-basic word is regarded as evidence of good word power, not as bad spelling.

This is not to say that sentences and spelling do not count at all. They should count and they do. The readers make a yes-or-no judgment about command of these skills from an analysis of the handling of sentences that begin with subject phrases or transitional elements and from an analysis of the spelling of grade-level words and the knowledge demonstrated of the spelling of common morphemes.

Research Findings

The validation process and subsequent research have produced many fascinating, useful findings. For example, an early finding of the validation study was that behavior in some of the primary traits, such as sentence sense, appears to have a significant positive relationship with the overall rating. Tendencies and relationships, however, do not convert to hard and fast evaluation criteria. The exceptions to the tendency need to be dealt with as surely as the papers that appear to fit the generalization. Construction of a scattergram highlights the mismatches farthest from the regression line and make it possible to revise the theory of relationship in a way which satisfactorily accounts for the discrepancies. The high correlation between sentence errors and the overall rating of the papers derives mainly from the fact that virtually all the papers rated in the area from Level 4 to Level 7 demonstrated adequate command of sentence sense. On the other hand, some papers with few or no sentence errors received low ratings as a result of other serious deficiencies. Command of sentence sense of itself, one may infer, does not produce or even contribute to quality in writing, but a lack of this skill apparently condemns a paper to a poor rating regardless of other good qualities it may have.

This research finding, like many others, is reflected in the evaluation model. Adequate command of sentence sense is an essential condition for a paper to be rated Level 4 or higher starting with the fourth grade.

A related research finding will be knowingly greeted by all Piaget fans and should be of comfort to teachers who lament the student proclivity for "forgetting" everything they have been taught. A direct application of the Piagetian theory of assimilation and accommodation can explain the otherwise frustrating behavior of students who keep on "forgetting" what a sentence is each year. A tracking of student skills from grade to grade demonstrates that many who appear to have learned what a sentence is in grade four seem to forget what they know as they extend their concept of sentence to more complex language environments in grade five. The implication is that teachers literally do have to keep right on teaching what a sentence is, at least through grade eight, not because students forget what they have been taught or because teachers in the lower grades haven't done a thorough job of teaching, but because students need room to apply and extend concepts.

Writing in Grade Two

The evaluation model, along with the other essential components necessary to the successful operation of a district-wide writing program, has accomplished what some would regard as a miracle in student achievement. One of the most rewarding, exciting outcomes of the entire effort is that no one has any idea yet what the achievable limits are.

Figure 9 illustrates the Level 5 criteria for grade two in a copy of a typical Level 5 paper illustrating the achievement level in terms of actual student performance.

The student who wrote the paper was designated as a Level 5 writer for being able to compose a completed series of ideas, and to use some non-basic constructions. The student did not regularly combine and embed sentences, which is the reason the competency level was not set at Level 6.

Much can be learned about what children know and how they learn by analyzing their miscues, for instance, the representations of money notation in this paper. This student knows that certain symbols are used to represent money values and that the symbol for dollar is placed in front of the value, although the child confuses the dollar symbol with the cent sign. As the sequence continues, the writer tries to express the money value in text instead of notation with *100 dollar* and then produces an amazing instance of child logic. If *100* represents one dollar, then *100.50* must be the way to express a dollar, fifty cents, even though an earlier passage expresses the value in more conventional terms as *¢1.50*.

Gr. 2

① The Lonely Bird

Once I was walking
down The sidewalk.
I came to a tree,
I saw a bird in it.
I said how are you?
He didn't anser me.
I ask him if he was
lonely.

②

He said ofcors.
H wanted me to be His
Friend.
I said to the Bird ok.
And he flue down on m-
y sholder.
I said I'll be wor best
friend.
So him and me went to

③

pet store.
To getsome bird seed, and
a cage.
We went to my house.
The bird was sining all
The way.
I said mom. mom look
at my pet she said how
much did pay

④

I said ¢1.50.
She said came the birds
cost ¢1:00 the cage cost
loo doller and the seeds
cost loo doller. I only
paid loo 50.
She said I ges you can-
kepp the Blue Jay for
a pet. the end

Figure 9. Sample paper illustrating the Level 5 criteria for evaluating second-grade writing.

In 1974, 10 percent of second graders were judged to have Level 5 skills or better. One year later, in 1975, after serious discussions with teachers who ignored the in-service training and who treated the curriculum guidelines that called for the teaching of writing in grades one and two as a silly new frill, 44 percent of second graders attained one of the top three levels. This achievement surpassed all expectations and was thought at the time to represent optimum achievement for the grade. In 1979, after four more years of experience, fully 96 percent of the second graders wrote papers as good as or better than *The Lonely Bird*, a level of achievement which was unimaginable in Grosse Pointe a few short years ago and still is unimaginable in the many school systems which do not have any idea what first and second graders can do with the right curriculum, an excellent faculty, and a good management system.

How well do second graders write? In 1979, 12 percent wrote papers like the one presented in Figure 10.

Note the consistent use of non-basic constructions and the complexity of structure:

> . . . lived a young bird.
> Roaming the sky looking for a friend. . . .
> . . . so he could find one or two friends.
> After a few long considering hours. . . .
> . . . it was decided that. . . .
> . . . as he packed. . . .
> . . . his suitcase he clutched. . . .
> . . . his hat plopped on his head. . . .

Note the use of specific words:

> roaming
> clutched
> plopped

The importance of such a program to a school system cannot be overstated. Virtually all students in Grosse Pointe enter the third grade able to compose a completed series of ideas about a topic with at least some use of non-basic constructions or transitions. Second-grade teachers are justly proud of their accomplishment, and third-grade teachers know they will inherit a group of students who expect to compose as a regular part of school activity and everyday living. Third-grade teachers do not have to teach skills in a vacuum to students who have had no experience composing. Their job is to help students continue to grow in the full, free expression of thought in writing while they help

Gr. 2
The Lonely Bird
Once on a meadow,
about a half a mile
from the nearest farm-
house, lived a young
bird.
Roming the sky looking
for a friend.
Every day he looked.

Finely he decited to
move closer to the
farmhouse so he could
find 1 or 2 friends.
After a few long
considering hours it.
was decited that the
next day was the day
to move.

The next day he
was up at dawn.
Today's the day he
sang out happily as
he packed.
Soon he was off,
his suitcase he cluched
in one wing, his hat
ploped on his head too

Very soon he was over a
cool lake.
Hmm? I think I'll
take a dip he siad
Hey there are other
birds there I've finely
found some friends.
And from then on he
was not a lonely bird.

Figure 10. Sample of second-grade writing in 1979.

students begin to learn to re-express their ideas in conventional orthography.

How Students Progress in High School

The true test of a system like this one is not whether it makes linguists happy or pleases second-grade teachers. Until one can see what happens to these second graders as they move through the grades and become high school students, the plan remains a theory, not a proven method, in the view of most observers. Fortunately, it is not necessary to wait eight more years. The evaluation model was extended to grades nine and ten and field tested for the first time in 1979. Even though the tenth graders about whom the data were collected began the new program in grade five, not grade one, and even though approximately 40 percent of the present class entered the school system after that time, the results are more than encouraging. Figure 8 presents the Level 5 criteria for grades nine and ten found in a copy of a typical Level 5 paper.

The introduction and conclusion are competently handled. The organization of the body is well-conceived with a paragraph about the immature ninth-grade boys, a paragraph about the silly, gaudy girls, and a paragraph about what the boys and girls are like when they all get together. The mechanics are competent for an impromptu, if not flawless. The word choices are lively, and the sentence structure is rich and varied. An abundance of detail is used to support the main points, and the writer holds some opinions about the topic which are expressed with vitality and sincerity.

It may not be too much to hope from this demonstration of competence that this writer—and the many tenth graders in the school system with equivalent or better abilities—should have little difficulty earning an A or B in first-year English in college or preparing a competent report or recommendation in the world of work. After all, the paper was a forty-five minute impromptu, not a prepared piece of writing, and the student still does have two years of instruction and experience remaining in high school English.

Parent groups which see slide presentations of student writing are delighted and astonished to see evidence that their fears about student achievement in writing are groundless. The typical reaction when seeing a slide of a Level 5 paper for grade ten is "That's wonderful! Why isn't it a 7?" The easiest way to explain the difference between a 5 and a 6 is to point out some things that the Level 5 writer could have done but didn't. A Level 6 student writing the paper in Figure 11 would have recognized that he or she is, after all, only a year removed from the so-called immaturity of the ninth graders who now look so silly and might also have added some wry commentary about what tenth graders must look like to juniors and seniors.

Fully 39 percent of tenth graders were placed on Levels 5, 6, or 7 in 1979 achievement testing. Even if the evaluation model had no other value at all, it produces incontrovertible documentation that the school system is not producing masses of functional illiterates. Local critics are totally disarmed by the evidence.

> The Typical Ninth Grader
> One can always tell a ninth grader from any other of the high schoolers. The ninth grade boys are immature, the ninth grade girls are constantly fighting for recognition by the upper class boys, and both ninth grade boys and girls attend mostly all the activities that the school girls.
>
> At lunch time, if you suddenly see a piece of pizza fly past your table, you are sure to know that it came from a cluttered table of immature ninth grade boys. You might turn your head to see where it came from and they will give you a look of complete inocence. The lunch lady will then stomp up to the table and say her usual, "Who threw that" and each boy will have his finger pointing to the other boy across the table. Well, it just goes to show you that anyone can tell a ninth grade boy from all the rest.

Figure 11. Sample paper illustrating the Level 5 criteria for evaluating tenth-grade writing.

Have you ever seen more girls trying to act more mature than they really are than those darling ninth grade girls? A year ago in eighth grade, some of them would never have thought there was such a thing as make-up! If you take one look around at a class full of ninth grade girls you will see that their face is hidden behind layers of make-up and a huge mop of curls plastered down by hairspray. They all must wear high heels with straight leg jeans to show that they can handle the strain of walking around school like that without tripping for a whole day! The funny thing is that the older boys still know that they are ninth graders.

Have you ever been to a dance or a basketball game or a football game without seeing the whole ninth grade class there? If you find there is nothing else to do after a basketball game on Friday night you decide to stay for the little dance after. You step onto the dance floor and you notice that there are tons of short boys standing off to one side and on the other side you see a quantity of restless, giggley girls. You realize that none of your friends are here so you figure your missing out on some great, wild party. So, you leave to find this crazy party and you discover that a Senior is having it. Well, you can almost guess that there will be a few ninth grade girls trying to mingle with the rest of the older crowd.

So you see, the ninth grade gang of smart mouthed, immature boys, along with the ninth grade flood of silly, gaudy girls are set apart from the rest of the world in a humorous way.

Figure 11. Continued.

Other Findings

During the short life of the Grosse Pointe writing project, many things have been learned about children, writing, and about learning itself. Each deserves a chapter of explanation and documentation, but are briefly outlined here.

Scores on standardized tests of usage and punctuation do not measure or predict performance in actual written expression.

First and second graders can learn to compose ideas in writing if one is willing to disregard spelling, punctuation, and capitalization.

If the right time for learning is not seized in a child's developmental history, the omission may be irreparable. Many students who do not learn to compose in the elementary grades may never learn to write competently. Little is known about how to correct this omission or about whether this omission is always correctible.

Students who enter the third grade able to compose a completed series of ideas about a topic become better writers than students who learn composing and skills at the same time.

Personal and imaginative expression is the mode of expression which best helps elementary students develop their competencies in written expression. Other forms of writing are desirable and necessary in a comprehensive language arts program, but personal writing is the best vehicle to help students use the full power of their "inner language."

If all or most students compose in stilted, basic sentences, something is terribly wrong with the teaching.

Each grade level plays an important role in helping students develop their writing abilities. No grade level and no school level can do the job by itself.

The seventh grade is plenty of time to start teaching "paragraph writing" and writing about expository topics.

A ten-thousand-student school system is not too big for a district-wide writing program to work.

A New Look at Research on Writing

Donald Graves
University of New Hampshire, Durham

Unfortunately, only 156 studies of writing in the elementary grades, or an average of six annually, have been done in the United States in the last twenty-five years.[1] Research on writing was in such low esteem from 1955–1972 that 85 percent of all studies were done exclusively as dissertations. Research on writing wasn't important enough for most doctoral advisors to consider conducting it themselves. Rather, it was an exercise allowing students to apply courses in statistics to their dissertations. Eighty-one percent of all dissertation research in this period involved experimental designs seeking to find "good methods" in the teaching of writing.

These figures came at a time in American education when most school money was spent on developing children's reading skills. For every $3,000 spent on children's ability to receive information, $1.00 was spent on their power to send it in writing.[2] The funds for writing research came to less than .10 percent of all research funds for education.

From 1955–1972, 68 percent of all research was concerned with what the teacher was doing in the classroom. We were so preoccupied with ourselves as teachers that only 12 percent of the studies were concerned with a look at what children did when they wrote.

The research conducted on best methods for teachers was of the worst type. We took the science model of research and attempted to remove certain variables from their context to explain

---

1. Studies were reviewed through ERIC, *Research in the Teaching of English, Elementary English, Language Arts,* and *Dissertation Abstracts.*

2. These data were taken from the Ford study, *Balance the Basics: Let Them Write,* by Donald H. Graves, and from surveys of public school spending on textbooks, personnel, and materials related to reading and writing.

two crafts, teaching and writing, by dismissing environments through statistical means. We tried to explain complex wholes and processes through "hard data" about variables removed from context.

We complained that teachers would not pay attention to research. But so far the teachers have been right—most of the research wasn't readable and was of limited value. It couldn't help them in the classroom. They could not see their schools, classrooms, or children in the data. Context had been ignored.

Context needs to be explained. When six-year-old Janet writes "reindrer" in the midst of the sentence, "All of the *reindrer* lovd him," the word falls in more than the context of a written syntactical unit. Janet sings, speaks, rereads, listens to her text as she composes this selection for the Christmas holidays. She draws after she writes, chats with other children about expectations of Christmas gifts, converses with the teacher. She writes in a room that encourages child publication, mutual child help, and the importance of personal voice and information. Within the context of Janet's own development, she has gone through three stages of invented spelling: first sounding letters, then writing consonants in initial and final positions, now borrowing from the visual memory systems contributed by reading.

In the broader ethnographic context, Janet's mother writes letters, is college educated and interested in her child's progress, and lives in a suburban-rural town of 8,500 in New England. Janet's teacher writes for publication. In Janet's school, the principal speaks, writes, and listens to the teachers. In turn, teachers know their ideas will be heard. Such contexts have been ignored in much of the past research related to writing.

More than half of all research on children's writing in the last twenty-five years has been done in the last seven, and only 42 percent of it by dissertation. This research has broadened to include advisors of research and other professionals. Interest in descriptive studies of children's activity has risen from 12 to 48 percent of all studies. The context of writing is beginning to be described, though very crudely. Experimental design studies of what teachers do have dropped to 40 percent of the total.

A new kind of research stimulated by Janet Emig's (1969) case study of the composing processes of twelfth graders has broadened the context of investigation. Her research and the research of Graves (1974, 1979–80) focused on what writers did *during* the composing process. Descriptions were also given of the contexts in which the data were gathered. Although this is a new research area in terms of a history of research on writing, there is growing interest by both researchers and teachers in the data coming from the studies.

Most case study research is still being done with older students, notably the work of Hayes-Flower (1978–79), Sommer (1979), and Perl (1979). Far more needs to be done with younger children. We need more information on child behaviors and decisions *during* the writing process, rather than just speculation on child activity during writing from written products alone.

Time, money, and personnel investments in writing have changed within the last three years. Great imbalances in attending to communication skills still exist, but there is more interest in the teaching of writing. Some of this has come through response to state-mandated testing which has been invoked or is on the drawing boards in almost all of the fifty states.

There is also more interest in writing because teachers are beginning to get more help with their own writing processes. It is less common now for teachers to be lectured about the writing process, discussing the skill out of context, unallied with an involvement with writing itself. Such programs as the Bay Area Writing Project and the Vermont Writing Program have had national effects through attention to the teacher's own writing. Teachers have begun to understand the nature and context of the writing process through their own writing. They now can view what children do within the framework of practicing the craft themselves.

These efforts have also spurred greater interest in research, but research that relates to teachers' new understandings of the context of the writing process. That is, teachers now know the meaning of rehearsal (prewriting), redrafting, and development of skills related to publication. They want to know more about research that provides information in which they can "see" the students and classrooms in which they teach.

Teachers want to become involved in research themselves. Those who write themselves, who have become interested in what children do when they write, want to know how they can participate in gathering their own information on children's writing.

Financial commitments to the improvement of writing are still unfortunately low. The National Institute of Education allocated funds for research in writing for the first time in 1977.

Requests for proposals for research in writing improvement were instituted two years later. We have gone from nothing to barely something in the provision of research funds. Far more funds have been expended on the assessment of writing achievement. Educational Testing Service, the National Commission on Education in the States, and most State Departments have allocated funds to find out how students are progressing in writing.

The eighties are a time of hope and optimism. Research in writing has such a short history that it is not yet weighed down by many of the traditions that plague most research in education. Research in education has attempted to make a science of predicting human behavior from one setting to another through statistically controlled experiments. From the outset, research in writing reflected the experimental approach but only recently has begun to break away through process-observational studies and a broadened context to include the study of child growth. It is just beginning to provide information that teachers in the classroom can use.

A Necessary Pattern of Development

We may lament that time has been wasted on experimental designs and on a preoccupation with self (what teachers ought to do), but this pattern of development was necessary, important, unavoidable. Children, teachers, researchers, develop in similar patterns. I went through the same process in learning to teach.

The first day I ever taught I could hear only the sound of my own voice. I stood back and listened with terror as I searched for the right words. My seventh-grade class was an audience that barely existed. My chief questions at that point were, "What do I say? What do I do?" I could scarcely hear students' responses to my questions. Plans written days before determined my actions, regardless of students' responses. Answers fit my questions on a one to one basis, or they were not worthwhile. I hardly knew what was coming from the blur of faces in front of me.

In time the faces became more distinctive. I even began to notice what students did after I asked questions, or directed them to an activity. But my main concern was to crank up the machinery of learning, set the children on a course, and hope they would reach some worthwhile port of acquiring knowledge. Like the young learners in my room, I was only concerned with the beginning and end of learning. Not much existed in between. "How do I get started? What do I do when the papers are completed?"

Children develop along similar lines: they hear and write the initial consonants of words, then final consonants. The interior portions of words hardly exist. In reading, information at the end and beginning of selections is the most easily recalled. In Piaget's simple directive to children to draw all the steps showing a pencil falling from a vertical to horizontal position, the children can only draw the initial (vertical) and final (horizontal) positions, with none of the intermediary stages sketched in. When children, adults, researchers first initiate activity, there are no middles, only beginnings and endings. In short, they have a very limited space-time understanding of the universe, not unlike my first days of teaching. Furthermore, they are so absorbed in the rightness of their own acts, they find it difficult to empathize with the points of others.

It wasn't until much later in my career that I was able to focus on what children were doing, in order to adjust my own teaching style. I found that I could not afford to be without the information that told me where they were. As a result, I began to participate in the "middle" of the process of their learning. For example, I asked questions while they were in the middle of observing the travel patterns of turtles. I responded to their initial observation notes, asking more questions. And back they went to add, delete, or otherwise revise their earlier observations.

It is encouraging to note similar development in research patterns over the past twenty-five years. We have moved from a preoccupation with self in teaching to more studies of children, and now the middle ground, the process of writing itself. The space-time factors of research have been expanded. Such trends must continue throughout the eighties; but we must continue to be wary of studies that reduce attention to the context of investigation.

Further Research Backgrounds

We look at recent history of research in writing so that past mistakes will not be repeated. We review this history to take stock, learn, and forge on. We have been slow to take heed of the warnings of significant researchers. Since the early twenties, one researcher after another has warned of the danger of fragmentary approaches to research in children's writing. Braddock (1968) observes that writing is an organic process that defies segmentation:

> Anyone who has read a considerable portion of the research in the teaching and learning of English composition knows how much it leaves to be desired. In the first major summary and critical analysis of the research, Lyman (1929) wrote that "a complex phenomenon such as composition quality seems to defy careful analysis into constituent parts" and noted that the pioneer studies he reviewed "measure pupil products and assume that by doing so they are evaluating the manifold intangible processes of the mind by which those products were attained." (p. 302)

Meckel (1963), Parke (1961), and Braddock (1963) called for research that focused more on learners than teachers. They called for studies on the writing process that involved longitudinal research. Such research was difficult, too time-consuming for doctoral students, and certainly defiant of conventional statistical interventions.

Problems with Experimental Design

Though they purport to give direct help, persons using experimental designs to conduct writing research have contributed least to the classroom teacher. They respond to questions teachers ask most: "How do I get the students to write? What will stimulate, motivate them into writing action? What is the best way to correct papers?" Typically, the research model will try three different stimuli to induce students to better writing. One group will receive "no treatment." If one method, usually the favorite method of the researcher, should receive better marks—that is, show with ninety-five to one odds or better that the good results in student writing from the chosen method were not due to chance—then the approach is purported as valid for other children and teachers. This is an attempt to show via scientific means that an exportable method for teaching children to write has been found. Independent of the philosophical issues involved with this approach to teaching writing, the basic issue of context remains.

We have tried to borrow science from other fields in order to apply it to the study of human behavior. In the fields of agriculture, chemistry, and medicine, practitioners cannot afford to be without the latest findings. Better strains of hybrid corn increase food production for millions; miracle drugs are synthesized and save lives. New processes for using chemicals are developed, saving millions of dollars for industry. Research in science delivers.

Research in education is not a science. We cannot transfer science procedures to social events and processes. We are not speaking of corn, pills, or chemicals when we speak of what people do when they write. Elliott Mishler (1979), in one of the most telling articles written on research in context, observes the domination of research by experimentation in the social sciences:

> Despite the philosophical critique of this traditional model of science, its application to human affairs has remained triumphant. Researcher methods based on this model, which can be referred to collectively as context-stripping procedures, are taught to us in our graduate schools and we become properly certified as educational researchers, psychologists, or sociologists when we can demonstrate our competent use of them in our dissertations. (p. 3)

Research about writing must be suspect when it ignores context or process. Unless researchers describe in detail the full context of data gathering and the processes of learning and teaching, the data cannot be exported from room to room.

Devoid of context, data become sterile. One of the reasons teachers have rejected research information for so long is that they have been unable to transfer faceless data to the alive, inquiring faces of the children they teach. Furthermore, the language used to convey these data has the same voiceless tone that goes with the projection of faceless information. The research is not written to be read. It is written for other researchers, promotions, or dusty archives in a language guaranteed for extinction.

Writing process research can help the classroom teacher with writing. It's just that this research cannot pretend to be science. This does not mean that research procedures cease to be rigorous when describing the full context of human behavior and environment. The human faces do not take away objectivity when the data are reported. The face emerges from enormous amounts of time spent in observing, recording, and analyzing the data. When the face emerges in the reporting, it comes from tough selection of the incident that represents a host of incidents in context.

Studies that expand the context of writing are expensive. Thousands of hours are required to gather the full data. Personnel costs are high. For this reason, better procedures need to be developed to save on research costs.

We can never forget that if information from one study is to be used in another teaching situation with other children, the most thorough description of contextual factors must be given. When the process and context are described in simple, straightforward language, teachers will be ready consumers of the information.

Teachers who read such information often want to try informal research projects of their own. Since the procedures were conducted in classrooms, they see themselves in the midst of the data along with the children. They begin to keep daily records of skills advancement along with collected writings of the children. Charts of daily child conferences and reading and writing growth patterns are observed and recorded. Much of these data are only one step away from formal research studies.

Research for the Eighties—What Do We Need?

Research on writing in the eighties must involve the fullest possible contexts. We can no longer have experimental or retrospective studies that move in with treatments of short duration, or that speculate on child growth and behaviors through a mere examination of written products alone. Contexts must be broadened to include closer and longer looks at children while they are writing. These contexts must be described in greater detail.

In this section on research needed for the eighties, a more detailed description of context will be given, then a listing of research questions about children, teachers, and writing environments. This will be followed by a discussion of new research designs and procedures.

A researcher's description of context is given within the confines of print, which is linear and segmented, word following word. Even careful description of context through words has its limitations, since words cannot portray the many systems and variables that operate *simultaneously* as children write. For example, as Chad writes we observe and infer the following *simultaneous* actions in a *four-second interval:*

1. Voices "shhh-t-n" (shooting)
2. Hears own voice
3. Leans toward page
4. Grips pencil between thumb and forefinger
5. Glances at drawing at top of paper and observes pencil operate between lines
6. Holds paper with left hand with paper slightly turned to the right of midline

7. Sits on edge of chair

8. Tips shoulder as if to feel action of gun (inferred)

9. May hear voice over intercom asking teacher a question

10. Produces mental imagery of man shooting (inferred)

11. Produces mental imagery of word "shooting" (inferred)

12. Feels friction of pencil on paper surface

To describe this in narrative even with the greatest of care may still involve the researcher in distorting the time-space dimensions of the actual events and the simultaneity of the events.

Another Look at Context

The meaning of any situation is contained in the context of the act. A fourteen-month-old child reaches several times for a ball beyond his grasp. In frustration, he utters "ba." The mother turns, notices his outstretched hand and shouts to her husband, "John, Andy just said 'ball,' isn't it wonderful!" If the parent had heard the utterance without observing the context, she would probably have had a different interpretation of the sounds. The full understanding of Andy's act is contained in expanding the time and space frame of investigation to include reviewing the child's previous utterances, uses of language with his parents, parent responses, the child's use of symbols, activities in shops, at grandparents', in clinics, or the broader communities in which such utterances develop. Even this brief expansion of contextual understanding is a simplification of many more complex ways of observing single acts. Studies of the growth and development of preschool children's oral language have paid far more attention to contexts than studies of children's growth in writing.

The understanding of any single written word demands similar expansion of the time-space frame of investigation. It is this time-space expansion that helps us understand the act of writing, as well as the designs and procedures needed to understand written acts.

A simplified description of what is meant by "context" of writing is given in three different contextual categories: (1) The Writing Episode, (2) The Life of the Child Who Writes, and (3) The Social-Ethnographic Context of the Episode. Each of these sections will be discussed through the life of one case, Chad. Following each section, questions will be raised for further study in the eighties.

The Writing Episode

Chad is a six-year-old first grade child who has been writing for only two weeks. When Chad writes "the grts," (the good guys), the message is barely decipherable, yet it contains a major breakthrough for him, since in this instance it is the first time he is able to read back his message. This is but a small part of Chad's writing episode. In this chapter, a writing episode is defined as encompassing all that a child does before, during, and after a single writing. Some of Chad's activity on the first line is shown in the following:

Line 1: Writing   the   g   r   t   s
Line 2: Oral
    Language   the   the   *guh*   guy   gut   t   "the gut guys"
                                                            rereads

The first line shows what letter the child actually wrote in relation to the second line, the language and sound supplied by the child as he wrote. Simultaneous to the writing, Chad supplies facial gestures and varying distances to the paper. He also changes his work as he goes. As a beginning writer he changes mostly at the point of sound-letter correspondence and the shapes of letters. He does not yet edit for syntactical or semantical fit. Chad also reads as he writes, another important contextual feature in the process. And he listens to what he hears in reading out loud to see if he is where he thinks he ought to be in the message. Writing for Chad is more complex than it seems.

The context of Chad's composing is understood further by going back to what he was doing just before he started to write. In this instance, he rehearsed (not consciously) for the writing act by drawing warfare between the "good guys" and the "bad guys" at the top of his paper. A series of action-reaction battles in the drawing were fought with eventual total destruction of everyone on the paper. When Chad was asked, "Tell me what you are going to write after you finish the drawing," he replied, "Wait and see." Broadening this context still further, data show that Chad answers with more complete information in the middle of drawing about what he will write. "Wait and see," is probably a staying action, the same as, "I don't know."

Chad rushes to the teacher when he finishes composing. Data show from other episodes that rushing to the teacher is an important sharing time for him. Chad stands next to the teacher where she is seated at the round table in the back of the classroom. His left arm presses against hers as he leans, points to the paper, speaks to her with his face but eighteen inches from hers as he explains the episode on the paper. He can read some of the words, but the crude spellings of several have led to an evaporation of meaning. Still, he can at least get help from the drawing to communicate the main action of his writing.

A simple review of Chad's written product would have given a very limited explanation of what had occurred in the writing episode. The functions of various acts, the trials, would not have been understood in the same way as the direct observation of the composing of the episode itself.

We are just beginning to get a sense of the ingredients within the writing episode, but far more data are needed to explain how children function. We particularly need the data to begin to develop a theory of writing as called for by Martha King (1978). The following questions are posed for research investigation in the eighties.

1. What is the nature and function of oral language as it accompanies the writing process? How does this change within individual cases? Who are the children who do not use language to accompany the writing process?

2. How does rehearsal change as children grow older? What is the nature of different rehearsals within a single child, across many children?

3. What is the nature of syntactical and semantical decisions *within* child revisions? How do these decisions change with subsequent revisions of the same selection? How do these decisions change over a series of years within one child, across children of different ages?

4. How do children use other children or the teacher to help them in their writing? How does this vary with different kinds of writers and in different environments?

5. What is the context in the episode in which children change spellings? When do spellings become established into a final form?

6. Under what circumstances do children reread their writing? What is the nature of the reading act in writing, especially the reading act in relation to revision?

7. How do children learn to use space on their paper when first writing or when doing advanced revisions? What are the changing spatial demands of writing?

8. Under what circumstances do children use conventions, change them and grow with them over the years? Are there certain ways in which children use information that demand a broader repertoire of conventions?

9. What types of hesitation, delay phenomena, are observed that might be connected with a concept of "listening" to the text?

10. What types of left-right brain activity are indicated in the child's functioning in the writing process?

The Broader Context of One Episode in a Life

One writing episode does not explain Chad's behavior. Other episodes are reviewed in relation to the one completed. The analysis of episodes reveals sequences of development over time. A simple example of a sequence is contained in children's general use of drawing in relation to writing. For most children, drawing precedes writing since the child needs to see and hear meaning through drawing. Later, as children know better what they will write, they illustrate *after* writing. In time, they do not need to draw at all. There are exceptions based on intra-differences and different functions for the drawing.

Other contextual data are needed from Chad's own background to better understand what he does in the writing episodes. For example, interviews with Chad's teachers and parents show that Chad did not speak understandable messages until he was approximately four years of age. For many months after entering school Chad could not write. He did not understand the relationship between sound and symbol. He could not read his first attempts to write. There were too few cues to read them the next day. Still, his drawings were filled with information. He spoke at length with other children about the content of his drawings.

Other contextual information from Chad's life gathered over time are the following: changing concept of good writing; function of writing; sense and use of audiences; range and type of topics chosen; use of person; characterizations; territorial involvement of content; problem solving strategies in such areas as blocks, science, mathematics, etc. Sequences of development in each of these informational areas have their own context—What came before? What will follow? The sequence and interrelationship of each scheme provides more context for explaining behaviors in any one aspect of the composing process. Much of these data come from product analysis, child, parent, and teacher interviews, and the analysis of writing episodes.

Far more needs to be done in these important areas. A child's changing concepts of the writing process are particularly difficult to gather from interviews and ultimately depend on data from child functioning within the writing process itself, as well as from extensive analysis of the writing product. The following questions for research in the eighties are related to background information needed to understand a child's writing process:

1. What is the relationship between children's concepts of the writing process and what they *do* during their writing?
2. What is the relationship between children's oral language and what they *do* during the writing process?
3. What is the relationship between children's processes of reading and how they read and revise their own texts?
4. What is the writer's topical range and use of genre over time?
5. How does the child use language to discuss the writing process? How does this change? How is this related to what the child does in the writing process?
6. What is the writer's process of composing in different content areas?
7. What is the *actual* audience range within the child's class-room, school, home? How does this relate to the child's concept of audience, use of audience?
8. How much autonomy does the child exercise in the writing process?
9. How do children change in making the transition from oral to written discourse?
10. What is the relationship between a child's influence on the writing of other children (topic, skill, text, aid) and the child's own performance within the writing process?

Ethnographic Context

Chad's writing is not done in a vacuum. He is part of a social context in which children, teachers, administrators, parents, and a community act on their values about writing. These values and practices affect what Chad does when he writes. They affect topic choice, interactions with other children, the teacher, his style of solving problems. It is difficult to know what aspects of the broader context affect the composing process, and the child's voice in the process. This is one of the least explored areas in writing research.

Examples of ethnographic research conducted in Chad's writing situation are the following.

1. *Communication Patterns.* Examine the contexts of Chad's writing by collecting and tracing written and oral communication along these routes: community, board of education, superintendent of schools, middle management, principal, teacher, Chad, and Chad's parents.

   The contents and values expressed in patterns would be classified and assessed, and the effects of those messages would be studied. They would also be assessed for open answers (solicited) vs. closed answers (directives without explanation or answers expected).

2. *Literacy Values.* How do adults in the same levels and routes mentioned in *Communication Patterns* practice and value their composing? What is the nature of the composing? What past experience in teaching has each had with learning to write? What, in fact, is the volume and type of their written communications?

Research Questions for Teachers

The teaching of writing needs major focus for the eighties, but we can no longer afford the errors of the past when experimental designs were used to study specific teaching methodologies. Our preoccupation with the correct stimulus for writing, correcting and grading final products, or with exercises to increase sentence complexity need to be abandoned. So much more is now known about the nature of the process itself, children's development as writers, and the importance of the context of writing that a new focus on the teacher is needed. Though much of our research has focused on teacher methodologies in the past, we have never actually studied the *process* of teaching writing. We have never studied even one teacher to know what ingredients are involved in teaching writing. Whereas the case study was the gateway to understanding the writing process and the ingredients involved in it, the same approach is now needed for the teaching process.

We are not starting from scratch. Extensive case studies of children writing put us ahead of where we were with the first case studies of children in 1973. Over the last two years, a research team from the University of New Hampshire has been observing the daily writing activity of young children. Because of the detailed focus on children through video and hand recording, there is an entirely different view of the importance and place of teaching. The situation is not unlike the artist who intently paints a landscape and becomes more acutely aware of the effect of weather on the emerging scene. The detailed observation of children is the beginning of understanding teaching, since teacher effects are seen more clearly in the context of child data. These kinds of data are also more easily reported to teachers since descriptions of the classroom, teacher activity, and the details of child activity before, during, and after composing are given.

The emphasis of the New Hampshire study, however, is on the child, with some data on teacher activity. The child still remains in context. Next studies need to focus on the teacher with peripheral data on the children. Extensive child data with transcripts of meetings with teachers suggest a host of questions that need to be researched in the future. None of these questions can be considered without spending time in the classroom and gathering data on both teachers and children, with full consideration given to what happens in the child's process of writing. Since more context is needed for understanding the research questions posed related to teaching, a two-column format is presented in Figure 12 with the research question in the first column, and discussion of hypotheses and preliminary data in the second.

Since so little data have been gathered on any of these questions, or on the process of teaching writing, the questions ought to be considered within the framework of case studies of competent teachers, those experienced in teaching writing, those willing to become involved in it for the first time. Detailed data gathering through video tapes, audio tapes, direct observation, and teacher and child interviews needs to be done. One of the best ways to gather the teacher case data is to do simultaneous case studies on children in the same environment. In this way the basic ingredients in teacher-child transactions can be examined more closely.

Research Designs and Procedures for the Eighties

Researchers in the eighties need to draw from many fields if they are to broaden the contexts of their investigations. Procedures from linguistics, anthropology, and developmental psychology need to work their way into the territories needing investigation. Educators ought to acquire more background in these fields. Similarly, educators need to invite specialists to become more acquainted with the process of education in public institutions.

What do teachers do when they confer with children about their writing?	We need to describe in detail what is contained in the effective writing conference. Also, teachers who are just starting to teach writing should be chosen so that their changing patterns of conferring with children can be recorded over time. We are speaking of case studies of specific teachers in a variety of settings.
How do teachers attend to children's papers in the writing conference?	Research conducted on this question will also respond to a host of other questions: (1) How specific is the writing conference? (2) How much did the teacher learn from the child in the conference. (3) How does the teacher give responsibility to the child, or take it away during the writing conference? (4) What is the relationship between the content of the writing conference and the child's subsequent activity in writing?
What is the number, frequency, and type of conference conducted in the classroom?	Very little is known about the patterns of teacher conferences with children. From our present study, we see conferences of from thirty seconds to twenty minutes duration. Conference patterns change, but what are those patterns?
How do teachers change what they attend to in the writing conference over a period of time?	We need to carefully monitor teacher changes with both experienced and inexperienced teachers, with different kinds of children. With some children it is more difficult to maintain ownership of the paper where it belongs, with the child. This question will make inroads on issues of match between teaching styles and child learning styles. Also, it may get at the question of match between teacher and child composing styles.
How does the teacher help children to help each other with their writing?	Teachers who enable children to help each other provide not only an important service in immediate child help, but a unique chance to learn more about writing by helping another person. Children in this situation are able to use language to talk about writing more specifically.

Figure 12. The relationship of research questions to current teaching practices.

	They come to the conference already primed to take more responsibility for their own writing content. The procedures that teachers use to help children to gradually take on more responsibility needs systematic study.
How does the teacher change the organization of the classroom to aid the writing of children?	Many organizational plans evolve as teachers gain experience in helping children to take more responsibility for their writing. The more choice and flexibility children have during the time for writing, the more structure and organization is needed. The process of providing a structure—first visible, then more invisible—need more systematic study.
What examples of writing are provided for children?	Children need to read the writing of others, and from the standpoint of their own authorship. The researcher questions: Is the writing provided the teacher's own? The child's own? Other children's? Writers from children's literature?
How much time is provided for writing?	The amount of time in relation to children's own writing episodes and patterns needs to be studied. What are the time provisions?
How does the teacher use writing across the curriculum and in different genre?	Writing cannot be contained by the personal narrative alone. Since it exists to clarify meaning, it applies across the curriculum. The breadth of genre and content needs to be examined in relation to time provided for writing, conference patterns, different types of children in the study.
How does the teacher provide for the permanency of writing?	Much writing should last—for the sake of the child, other children, parents, and the teacher. This question examines ways in which teachers provide for writing pemanency through publications, collections of writing, writing folders, charts, etc.

Figure 12. Continued.

Research teams ought to be more interdisciplinary. A review of research in the last twenty-five years shows how insular research on writing has become. In the past, the only persons to serve on doctoral committees outside of education departments were statisticians and linguists.

I am not advocating that this research be turned over to outside specialists. The locus of research control must still remain with the educator who knows the context of the public school setting.

Design and Procedures

Depth needs to be added through different use of case, experimental, and ethnographic procedures *within the same study*. In short, the space-time dimensions of research must be expanded to include procedures in the same study that in the past have been used solely for one type of study alone. An example of such a study focusing on children is contained in Figure 13.

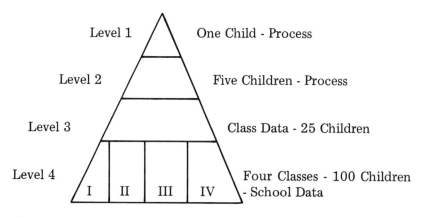

Figure 13. Design illustrating space-time dimensions of research.

In such a design, data are gathered simultaneously at four levels of investigation: intensive process data through direct observation of the child at Levels 1 and 2 over at least one year's time, and the full context of writing episodes are gathered from before the child writes until the child has had a response to the product. The child in Level 1 is a writer who gives more than the usual amount of information, involves a broader spectrum of development, and therefore merits more time from the researcher. Level 3 data come from the entire class in which Level 1 and 2 children reside.

Some informal observations are taken from them but all of their products are classified or duplicated for examination. Finally, product analysis is applied to four classes within the same school building, including each of the first three levels of the study. In this way, product analyses of larger groups can be further investigated for their process implications in the case study data. Similarly, case data variables that appear to be pivotal can be examined through interventions or product analyses at Levels 3 and 4. To date, three studies have been done in this manner: Graves (1973)(1979–80) and Calkins (1980).

Depth must be added through more intensive case studies with intra-differences (within the child differences) explained through one case. One child's behavior is described within the context of at least one to three years. In this way, the pattern of development within one variable or across variables can be examined and explained over a much longer period of time. Too often research contributes to a lottery philosophy of educating. That is, we look for similarities across children, ways of generalizing one child's behavior to aid other children. There is a value in this, but there is also a grave, potential weakness. We will look too quickly to see why the child before us is *the same* as other children rather than look at how the child is different. Or, if the difference is located, we seek to extinguish it in order to integrate the child into a homogeneous mass for more convenient instruction.

In short, we tend to overlook the one thing that makes the child different, unique. We tend to overlook the voice—the one experience or knowledge area the child knows well. Good teachers have responded to this uniqueness on an intuitive basis for years. Research needs to document intra-differences of the components that make children unique. Glenda Bissex (1980), in her study of of Paul over a five-year period, conducted this type of study. Also, the child in Level 1 (Figure 13) is a potential type for study of intra-differences. Data gathered in such depth usually point the way to discovering new variables not seen in the larger data gathering. We cannot afford to be without such studies.

How Will Research on Writing Influence the Eighties?

In the past, teachers have been excluded from the process of writing research. If this practice continues, then every recommendation written in this chapter won't make any difference. The base of research involvement must be broadened to include an active role by the public school teacher. When teachers become involved in research, researchers not only gather better data, but the context of research—the public school classroom—is enriched by the study itself. Teachers and researchers ought to know each other better for the sake of research and the children.

We need to dispel the mystique of research. For too long it has been maintained through irrelevant, context-stripping designs, and a language intended only for other researchers. It is even sometimes doubtful if the intended audience of professionals understands the language any better than the perplexed classroom teacher.

Teachers need to write. They not only need to write in order to understand the process they teach, but they also need to put into print their thoughts about the teaching of writing. Teachers who write will be different consumers of research information.

Even with the work of the Bay Area Writing Project, in which a great stress is placed on the development of the teacher's own writing, there is scant opportunity for teachers to develop their own skills in the writing process. People who teach a craft must practice it. It would be unheard of for a teacher of piano to never play, or a ceramicist to say to a class, "Here is the wheel, throw the clay," without first demonstrating what the teacher practices daily. Teachers don't need to become professional, publishing writers, but they do need to be acquainted with the craft at a personal, practical level.

Researchers in Residence—A Case Study

In the fall of 1978 three researchers began to observe children in the elementary schools of Atkinson, New Hampshire. They were there to observe: "How and in What Order Children Develop as Writers." The two-year grant from the National Institute of Education focused on children, not teachers. The team resisted requests for formal writing workshops with the staff. The researchers would only answer teacher questions about their children or the writing process.

The researchers had all been teachers and were published writers. Over coffee, at lunch, at breaks when gym, art, and music were taught, teachers asked questions about their children and the relation of the data to their teaching. The teachers controlled the questions, when they used answers, and the teaching of writing in their classrooms. The researchers did not have a writing program.

In a short time the mystique of "research and researcher" were removed. Researchers were just as perplexed as teachers about certain children. From the beginning, the researchers wrote, shared findings with the teachers, and published. Teachers could see that they often knew more about their own children than the researchers. Nevertheless, both teachers and researchers learned from the children.

Teachers began to write. They demanded an in-service course in both writing and the teaching of writing. An outside consultant worked with the teachers. Two of the teachers took formal courses in writing. Gradually, most of the staff of fourteen teachers worked on their own writing. More importantly, the teachers began to collect their own information about the children. Researchers kept charts of data about the children, and shared them with the teachers. Teachers, in turn, began to keep their own charts, their own data systems, and from these data to write articles of their own.

Most of the teachers involved keep extensive records, the base of good data for their own research. One teacher records the content of each writing conference, the patterns of spelling as children change throughout the year; another records the changing strategies of a child who has great difficulty in writing. They write about their information in such a way that they *show* other teachers what they do, as well as the data on which their judgments are based. Some of these recordings and methods were contained in the earlier chapter on classroom teaching practices.

The status of these teachers has changed. They have become a community since they have shown the nature of that community through their writing. They share stories about their own children, orally and in writing; they teach each other just as their children teach them, and they teach their administrator as well.

In a time when there is a shortage of teaching energy, these teachers even find the energy to write about what they are doing. They can do this because they have placed the responsibility for writing where it belongs, with the children. They believe that it is the child's responsibility to teach them about what they know. They help the child through extensive listening, confirmation, and questioning to share personal experiences, stories the child wishes to share. When children lead, and teachers listen, not only is there a new professionalism with the child, but the teacher (with the child speaking and supplying the energy) has time to write down the information children share. When children must assume a greater responsibility for information, drafting, and proofing, teachers in turn have the energy to publish and to review the data they have from conferences. Once teachers begin this approach to gathering information, they soon learn they cannot do without it.

When these teachers listen, gather data, write about it, share it with other teachers, and travel to other communities for workshops, they read research with a different voice. Researchers, whether informal data gathering, small action projects, or yearlong classifications of children's writing themes, are critical, active consumers of what happens in the field. They are interested in what is happening in their territory, what affects them. Furthermore, since they observe children and their own actions in relation to them, they have a different view of theory. They realize that basic research on children's writing and development and the theories of writing that emanate from the data are grounded in real children. They can be of help to them in their work with children, not ten years from now, but tomorrow.

Not every system can have full-time researchers in its midst. There are few grants given by the National Institute of Education; but there is a middle ground that researchers, teachers, and administrators can examine together that will give a new focus to the teaching of children and research for the eighties.

Professors of education need to spend more time in the only true laboratories, public school classrooms to understand the role of teacher and the processes of learning. Perhaps the reason researchers have neglected issues of context of learning in research for so long is that so little time has been spent on the sites where experimental data have been gathered. Whether by doctoral students, psychologists, or professors of education, research has been gathered in absentia.

There are several options that local school systems and universities can consider together. The success of the proposed ventures is dependent on both professors and teachers learning from children together. It is only the information they have in common about the children, the writing they do together, that will determine the development of a research community.

The following suggestions should aid cooperation between universities and school systems in the eighties.

1. Professors of education need to take more sabbaticals on site with teachers and children. Joint research projects can benefit teachers, professors, and the local school system.

2. Teachers can gather their own data during writing conferences, or review data patterns from children's writing collections. Many teachers have data that are very close to full research studies.

3. Teachers can relieve each other to observe children during breaks. These are breaks that make a professional difference; they supply a different kind of energy.

4. School systems can hire resident writing professionals whose main task will be to "live in" selected classrooms and provide data about responding to children's writing. The resident professional must be both writer and researcher. This person will not only work with the staff on their own writing, but share data on the writing processes of children as they aid the teacher whom they serve.

Final Reflections

In the past, research has been done at too rapid a pace. We can no longer zoom in on a research site, emerge like green berets from a helicopter, beat the bushes for data, and retire to ivy-covered sanctuaries. Sadly, an increasing number of school systems have marked their schools as "off limits" to researchers—with good reason. Researchers, like poor campers, have not left their sites more improved than when they arrived. Pre- and post-test data have been gathered, a six-week intervention introduced, and the final data not reported to the school system. Administrators and boards express their feelings directly: "We don't want any researchers experimenting on our kids."

Research that ignores context tends to be done in a hurry, to avoid the human issues of the persons involved in the study.

Research that broadens the base of context is automatically slower. Rarely is the study less than a full year. Although there are interventions included in the data gathering, much time is spent in describing children, teachers, the research site. Researchers spend months in advance of data gathering becoming acquainted with staff and in making it possible for the staff to get to know them. If researchers are to be guests in the classroom of the teachers, the teachers had better know their guests' values and habits.

Our experience in the New Hampshire study indicates that persistent, thorough, yet slow-paced data gathering has influenced the pace of teaching in the classroom. The teacher slows down and listens to the children, responds differently to the child's written drafts. Full descriptions of context of child, family, and school make them aware of many other processes operating on the child's behalf. Finally, teachers are able to focus far more on what children *can do*. Researchers and teachers alike share in the amazement of child potential.

Perhaps the focus of research in the eighties ought to be slow down, look at the full context of writing, and get to know the real potential of both children and teachers.

Writing in Grades One through Eight: Summary Reflections

Shirley M. Haley-James
Georgia State University, Atlanta

Invited guests still come to Suzanne Prince's classroom to be interviewed by her students. The first year that her interviewing-based oral language, listening, writing, and reading program was a part of her language arts curriculum, the children conducted their first interview in April. The second year she started the program in February, and the third year the interviews began in the Fall.

Each year, Suzanne's perceptions of when young children could learn to write had to be adjusted to accommodate new evidence. Her first graders' language learning and the development of their writing skills accelerated beyond her expectations at whatever point she initiated and supported their meaning-based communication about personal interests and experiences. She continues to build her writing program around learning experiences that prompt the desire to write, and in her classroom, writing now begins when the students enter first grade.

In an urban seventh-grade classroom far removed from the rural location of Suzanne's school, Robert Bostwick, who meets five classes of twelve-year-old students each day, pauses by the desk of Jenny Howard and listens to the new draft of her story about receiving a silver dollar from her beloved grandfather.

"Jenny, I can *see* here in your second paragraph how you felt when you opened the shiny blue box and he watched you take out the dollar. Are you going to go on developing your paper around how you feel about your grandfather?"

Jenny nods, but already her eyes show that she has stepped back in time to recapture some other image or memory that she wants to include in her paper. Mr. Bostwick moves on to respond to the work of another student and allows Jenny's recollections to develop naturally.

Suzanne Prince and Robert Bostwick teach writing differently now than they have in the past. Neither felt secure during the first few weeks of using a new approach, but then, neither had felt satisfied with approaches previously used. Both knew within a few weeks of starting their new programs that they were doing a better job of helping students with their writing than they had done before.

What makes the work of these teachers and that of others who are successfully teaching written composition in grades one through eight succeed? Each of their writing programs is as different as the personal perceptions and experiences of the teacher who has fashioned it. These inherent differences bring up the intriguing question, "In what ways are good elementary level writing teachers and their instructional programs *alike?*"

Perhaps certain observations about these teachers and their methods and programs will help resolve that question.

First, discontent with the effects of present teaching practices and programs has driven these teachers to find a better way of teaching. They question what they have been doing and probe what others whom they regard as successful are doing. A need to meet their students' needs and to help them develop their potential is central to their work.

Second, though each of their programs differs, all are based on the belief that children improve their writing when writing experiences are based on the drive to communicate. Successful writing teachers assume that every child has not one, but many things, to write about, and that every child can achieve satisfaction from communicating personal meaning through writing.

Third, writing has become personally important to these teachers and they find time for children in their classrooms to write regularly. Learning-by-doing is not a euphemism to them; time for writing is a priority in their programs.

Fourth, these teachers continue to grow professionally. They are concerned with unveiling the magic of a child's mind brought to life by the need to tell, or the joy in telling, through writing. Thus, they push on beyond every successful teaching experience to learn something else about teaching writing. They read, talk to other teachers, try other new approaches in their classrooms, and frequently participate in some way in research related to their work.

Helping children with their writing is an energizing goal that has become a passion for such teachers. They change their teaching as time passes because they pay attention to what works and does not work with their students. As these teachers grow and change as teachers of writing, the eleven observations about effective writing instruction and writing programs listed in Chapter 1 are made manifest in their instructional decisions.

These are ways in which good elementary level writing teachers and their instructional programs are alike. These are the teachers who teach written composition well.

References

Ballou, Frank W. *Scales for the Measurement of English Compositions* (The Harvard-Newton Bulletins, no. 2). Cambridge, Mass.: 1914.

Bissex, Glenda. *Gnys at Wrk: A Child Learns to Write and Read.* Cambridge, Mass.: Harvard University Press, 1980.

Braddock, Richard. "Composition." *Encyclopedia of Educational Research*, 1968.

Braddock, Richard, Lloyd-Jones, Richard, and Schoer, Lowell. *Research in Written Composition.* Urbana, Ill.: National Council of Teachers of English, 1963.

Breed, S. B. and Frostic, F. W. "Scale for Measuring the General Merit of English Composition." *Elementary School Journal* 17 (1917): 307–325.

Britton, James. "Now That You Go to School." In *Children and Writing in the Elementary School: Theories and Techniques.* Richard L. Larson, ed. New York: Oxford University Press, 1975.

Britton, James. "The Student's Writing." In *Explorations in Children's Writing.* Eldonna L. Evertts, ed. Urbana, Ill.: National Council of Teachers of English, 1970.

Burgess, Carol and others. *Understanding Children Writing.* Baltimore: Penguin Books, 1973.

Burrows, Alvina T. "Children's Writing and Children's Growth." *Elementary English* 28 (1951): 205–208.

Burrows, Alvina T. "Spelling and Composition." *Education* 79 (1958): 211–218.

Burrows, Alvina T. "Writing as Therapy." *Elementary English* 29 (1952): 135–138. Reprinted in *Issues and Problems in the Elementary Language Arts.* Walter T. Petty, ed. Boston: Allyn & Bacon, 1968.

Burrows, Alvina T. "The Young Child's Writing." In *Explorations in Children's Writing.* Eldonna L. Evertts, ed. Urbana, Ill.: National Council of Teachers of English, 1970.

Burrows, Alvina T., Monson, Diane R., and Stauffer, Russell G. *New Horizons in the Language Arts.* New York: Harper and Row, 1972.

Burrows, Alvina T. and others. *They All Want to Write.* 3rd ed. New York: Holt, Rinehart & Winston, 1964.

Calkins, Lucy McCormick. "Andrea Learns to Make Writing Hard." *Language Arts* 56 (1979): 569–576.

Calkins, Lucy McCormick. "Children Learn the Writer's Craft." *Language Arts* 57 (1980): 207–213.

Calkins, Lucy McCormick. "Children's Rewriting Strategies." To be published by *Research in the Teaching of English.*

Calkins, Lucy McCormick. "Punctuate! Punctuate? Punctuate." *Learning Magazine* 8 (1980): 86, 87–89.

Carlson, Ruth Kearney. *Writing Aids Through the Grades.* New York: Teachers College Press, 1970.

Carpenter, George R., Baker, Franklin T., and Scott, Fred N. *The Teaching of English in the Elementary and Secondary School.* New York; Longmans, Green & Co., 1908.

Cazden, Courtney. "Suggestions from Studies of Early Language Acquisition." *Childhood Education* 46 (1969): 127–131.

Clay, Marie. *What Did I Write?* Auckland, New Zealand: Heinemann Educational Books, 1975.

Commission on Composition of the National Council of Teachers of English. "Composition: A Position Statement." *Elementary English* 52 (1975): 194–196.

Commission on the English Curriculum of the National Council of Teachers of English. *Curriculum Series, Volume I, (The English Language Arts).* New York: Appleton-Century-Crofts, 1952.

Committee on Basic Aims of the National Council of Teachers of English. "Basic Aims for English Instruction in American Schools." *English Journal* 31 (1942): 40–55.

Committee on Writing Standards of the National Council of Teachers of English. *Standards for Basic Skills Writing Programs.* Urbana, Ill.: National Council of Teachers of English, 1979.

Cooper, Charles R. "An Outline for Writing Sentence-Combining Problems." *English Journal* 62 (1973): 96–102.

Cooper, Charles R. "Holistic Evaluation of Writing." In *Evaluating Writing: Describing, Measuring, Judging.* Charles R. Cooper and Lee Odell, eds. Urbana, Ill.: National Council of Teachers of English, 1977.

Cooper, Charles R. "Teaching Writing by Conferencing." In *Survival Through Language: The Basics and Beyond.* Rita Bean, Allen Berger, and Anthony Petrosky, eds. Pittsburgh: School of Education, University of Pittsburgh, 1977.

Cooper, Charles R. and Odell, Lee, eds. *Research on Composing: Points of Departure.* Urbana, Ill.: National Council of Teachers of English, 1978.

Cooper, Charles R. and others. "Tonawanda Middle School's New Writing Program." *English Journal* 65 (1976): 56–61.

Dawson, Mildred A. "Building a Language-Composition Curriculum in the Elementary School." *Elementary English Review* 8 (1931): 75–78, 94.

Dawson, Mildred A. "Children Need to Write." *Elementary English* 33 (1956): 80–83.

Dawson, Mildred A. "Guiding Writing Activities in the Elementary School." *Elementary English Review* 23 (1946): 80–83, 97.

Dawson, Mildred A. "Maximum Essentials in English." *Elementary English Review* 25 (1948): 35–38, 63.

Dawson, Mildred A. and others. *Guiding Language Learning.* New York: Harcourt, Brace & World, 1963.

Diederich, P. B. "How to Measure Growth in Writing Ability." *English Journal* 55 (1966): 435-449.

Driggs, Howard R. *Our Living Language: How to Teach It; How to Use It.* Lincoln, Neb.: The University Publishing Company, 1923.

Edmund, N. R. "Writing in the Intermediate Grades." *Elementary English* 36 (1959): 491-501.

Elkind, David. "Cognitive Development and Reading." In *Theoretical Models and Processes of Reading.* 2nd ed. Harry Singer and Robert B. Russell, eds. Newark Del.: International Reading Association, 1976.

Elley, W. B., Barham, I. H., Lamb, H., and Wyllie, M. "The Role of Grammar in a Secondary School English Curriculum." *New Zealand Journal of Education Studies*, May 1975: 26-42.

Emig, Janet A. "Components of the Composing Process Among Twelfth Grade Writers." Unpublished doctoral dissertation, Harvard University, 1969.

Emig, Janet. "Writing as a Mode of Learning." *College Composition and Communication* 28 (1977): 122-128.

Esbensen, Barbara Juster. *A Celebration of Bees: Helping Children Write Poetry.* Minneapolis: Winston Press, Inc., 1975.

Evertts, Eldonna L. "Components of Writing." In *Explorations in Children's Writing.* Eldonna L. Evertts, ed. Urbana, Ill.: National Council of Teachers of English, 1970.

Gentry, J. Richard and Henderson, Edmund H. "Three Steps to Teaching Beginning Readers to Spell." *The Reading Teacher* 31 (1978): 632-637.

Gerbrandt, Gary. *An Idea Book for Acting Out and Writing Language K-8.* Urbana, Ill.: National Council of Teachers of English, 1974.

Golub, Lester S. "How American Children Learn to Write." *Elementary School Journal* 74 (1974): 236-247.

Goodman, Kenneth and Goodman, Yetta. "Learning to Read Is Natural." Paper presented at Conference on Theory and Practice of Beginning Reading Instruction, Pittsburgh: April 13, 1976.

Graves, Donald H. *Balance the Basics: Let Them Write.* New York: The Ford Foundation, 1978.

Graves, Donald H. "Children's Writing: Research Directions and Hypotheses Based Upon an Examination of the Writing Processes of Seven-Year-Olds." Ph.D. dissertation, State University of New York at Buffalo, 1973.

Graves, Donald H. "An Examination of the Writing Processes of Seven Year Old Children." *Research in the Teaching of English* 9 (1975): 227-241.

Graves, Donald H. "The Growth and Development of First Grade Writers." Paper presented at Canadian Council of Teachers of English Annual Meeting, Ottawa, Canada: May 10, 1979.

Graves, Donald H. "Language Arts Textbooks: A Writing Process Evaluation." *Language Arts* 54 (1977): 817-823.

Graves, Donald H. "Let Children Show Us How to Help Them Write." *Visible Language* 13 (1979): 16-28.

Graves, Donald H. "Let's Get Rid of the Welfare Mess in the Teaching of Writing." *Language Arts* 53 (1976): 645–651.

Graves, Donald H. "We Won't Let Them Write." *Language Arts* 55 (1978): 635–640.

Graves, Donald H. "What Children Show Us About Revision." *Language Arts* 56 (1979): 312–319.

Graves, Donald H. "What Is Basic to Language." Speech presented at the IRA Convention, Houston: May 5, 1978.

Greene, Harry Andrew. *A Criterion for the Course of Study in the Mechanics of Written Composition.* Iowa City: University of Iowa Studies in Education Series, vol. 8, no. 4, 1933.

Greene, Harry Andrew and Petty, Walter T. *Developing Language Skills in the Elementary School.* 5th ed. Boston: Allyn & Bacon, 1975.

Greene, Harry Andrew and others. "Elementary School Subjects: English Language." *Review of Educational Research* 7 (1937): 474–481, 554–557.

Groff, Patrick. "Children's Oral Language and Their Written Composition." *Elementary School Journal* 78 (1978): 180-191.

Hailey, Jack. *Teaching Writing K-8.* Berkeley: University of California at Berkeley, 1978.

Haley-James, Shirley M. and Hobson, Charles David. "Interviewing: A Means of Encouraging the Drive to Communicate." *Language Arts* 57 (1980): 497–502.

Halliday, M. A. K. "Learning How to Mean." In *Foundations of Language Development*, vol. 1, pp. 239–265. Eric Lennenberg and Elizabeth Lennenberg, eds. New York: Academic Press, 1975.

Hatfield, W. Wilbur. "A Quick Look Back." *English Journal* 49 (1960): 517–519.

Hatfield, W. Wilbur. *An Experience Curriculum in English: A Report to the Curriculum Commission of the National Council of Teachers of English.* New York: D. Appleton-Century Co., 1935.

Hayes, Richard and Flower, Linda. "A Cognitive Model of the Writing Process." National Institute of Education Grant, 1978–1979.

Hillegas, M. B. "Scale for the Measurement of Quality in English Composition by Young People." *Teachers College Record of Columbia University*, September 1912.

Hosic, James Fleming. "Reorganization of English in Secondary Schools." A Report of the National Joint Committee on English Representing the Reorganization of Secondary Education of the National Education Association and the National Council of Teachers of English. *U.S. Education Bulletin*, no. 2, 1917.

Hoyt, F. S. "The Place of Grammar in the Elementary Curriculum." *Teacher's College Record* of Columbia University, November 1906.

Hudelson, Earl. *Hudelson English Composition Scale.* New York: World Book Company, 1921.

Hudelson, Earl. "Standards for the Measurement of English Composition in the Bloomington Indiana Schools." *English Journal* 5 (1916): 590–597.

Hunt, Kellog W. "Early Blooming and Late Blooming Syntactic Structures."

In *Evaluating Writing: Describing, Measuring, Judging*. Charles R. Cooper and Lee Odell, eds. Urbana, Ill.: National Council of Teachers of English, 1977.

Ilg, Frances and Ames, Louise Bates. *Child Behavior from Birth to Ten*. New York: Harper and Row, 1955.

King, Martha. "Research in Composition: A Need for Theory." *Research in the Teaching of English* 12 (1978): 193-203.

Klapper, Paul. *The Teaching of English: Teaching the Art and the Science of Language*. New York: D. Appleton & Co., 1916.

LaBrant, Lou. "The Individual and His Writing." *Elementary English* 27 (1950): 261-265.

LaBrant, Lou. "Inducing Students to Write." *English Journal* 44 (1955): 70-74, 116.

LaBrant, Lou. "Writing Is Learned by Writing." *Elementary English* 30 (1953): 417-420.

Leonard, Sterling Andrus. "As to the Forms of Discourse." *English Journal* 3 (1914): 201-211.

Leonard, Sterling Andrus. *English Composition as a Social Problem*. Cambridge, Mass.: Houghton Mifflin, 1917.

Leonard, Sterling Andrus. "In Praise of Prevision." *English Journal* 4 (1915): 500-507.

Leonard, Sterling Andrus. "On Setting Up Composition Targets." *English Journal* 8 (1919): 401-411.

Lloyd-Jones, Richard. "Primary Trait Scoring." In *Evaluating Writing: Describing, Measuring, Judging*. Charles R. Cooper and Lee Odell, eds. Urbana, Ill.: National Council of Teachers of English, 1977.

Lopate, Phillip. "Helping Young Children Start to Write." In *Research on Composing: Points of Departure*. Charles R. Cooper and Lee Odell, eds. Urbana, Ill.: National Council of Teachers of English, 1978.

Lundsteen, Sara W. *Help for the Teacher of Written Composition (K-9): New Directions in Research*. Urbana, Ill.: National Conference on Research in English and ERIC Clearinghouse on Reading and Communication Skills, 1976.

Lyman, R. L. "English Grammar in American Schools Before 1850." *Bulletin*. Department of the Interior, Bureau of Education, 1921.

Lyman, R. L. *The Enrichment of the English Curriculum*. Chicago: University of Chicago Press, 1932.

Lyman, Rolla O. *Summary of Investigation Relating to Grammar, Language and Composition*. Chicago: University of Chicago Press, 1929.

McKee, Paul. "An Adequate Program in the Language Arts." In *Teaching Language in the Elementary School: The 43rd Yearbook of the USSE, Part II*. Nelson B. Henry, ed. Chicago: University of Chicago Press, 1944.

Mearns, Hughes. *Creative Youth: How a School Environment Set Free the Creative Spirit*. Garden City, N.Y.: Doubleday, Page and Company, 1926.

Meckel, Henry C. "Research on Teaching Composition." *Handbook of Research on Teaching*. American Education Research Association, Chicago: Rand, McNally, 1963.

Mishler, Elliott. "Meaning in Context: Is There Any Other Kind?" *Harvard Educational Review* 49 (1979): 1-19.

Moffett, James. "I, You, and It." In *Children and Writing in the Elementary School.* Richard L. Larson, ed. New York: Oxford University Press, 1975.

Moffett, James. "Integrity in the Teaching of Writing." *Phi Delta Kappan* 61 (1979): 276-279.

Moffett, James. *A Student-Centered Language Arts Curriculum Grades K-13: A Handbook for Teachers.* Boston: Houghton Mifflin, 1968.

Moffett, James. *Teaching the Universe of Discourse.* Boston: Houghton Mifflin, 1968.

Murray, Donald M. "Internal Revision: A Process of Discovery." *Research on Composing: Points of Departure.* Charles R. Cooper and Lee Odell, eds. Urbana, Ill.: National Council of Teachers of English, 1978.

Murray, Donald M. "Teach the Motivating Force of Revision." *English Journal* 67 (1978): 56-60.

Murray, Donald M. "Write Research to Be Read." Special report to the Ford Foundation, 1977.

Murray, Donald M. *A Writer Teaches Writing: A Practical Method of Teaching Composition.* Boston: Houghton Mifflin, 1968.

Murray, Donald M. "The Writing Conference." Speech Presented at Georgia State University: May 2, 1979.

Murray, Donald M. "The Writing Process." In *Classroom Practices in Teaching English, 1973-1974: Language Activities.* Allen Berger and Blanch Hope Smith, co-chairpersons. Urbana, Ill.: National Council of Teachers of English, 1973.

Murray, Donald M. "Why Teach Writing and How?" *English Journal* 62 (1973): 1234-1237.

National Conference on Research in English. "Criteria of Excellence in Teaching the Language Arts." In *Teacher Effectiveness in Elementary Language Arts: A Progress Report.* Alan H. Robinson and Alvina T. Burrows, eds. Urbana, Ill.: National Conference on Research in English and ERIC Clearinghouse, 1974.

Noyes, E. C. "Progress in Standardizing the Measurement of Composition." *English Journal* 1 (1912): 532-536.

Odell, Lee. "Measuring Changes in Intellectual Processes as One Dimension of Growth in Writing." In *Evaluating Writing: Describing, Measuring, Judging.* Charles R. Cooper and Lee Odell, eds. Urbana, Ill.: National Council of Teachers of English, 1977.

Odell, Lee. "Question-Asking and the Teaching of Writing." *The English Record* 27 (1976): 78-86.

O'Donnell, R. C. "Reading, Writing and Grammar." *Education* 84 (1964): 533-537.

Parke, Margaret B. "Composition in Primary Grades." In *Children's Writing: Research in Composition and Related Skills.* Urbana, Ill.: National Council of Teachers of English, 1961.

Paul, Rhea. "Invented Spelling in Kindergarten." *Young Children* 31 (1976): 195-200.

Perl, Sondra. "The Composing Processes of Unskilled College Writers." *Research in the Teaching of English* 13 (1979): 317-336.

Petty, Walter T. and Jensen, Julie M. *Developing Children's Language.* Boston: Allyn and Bacon, 1980.

Petty, Walter T., Petty, Dorothy C., and Becking, Marjorie F. *Experience in Language.* 2nd ed. Boston: Allyn and Bacon, 1976.

Planning Commission of the National Council of Teachers of English in Conjunction with the Basic Aims Committee. "The Function of English in Wartime." *English Journal* 31 (1942): 91-109.

Pooley, R. C. "Grammar in the School of Today." *English Journal* 43 (1954): 142-146.

Pooley, R. C. "What Grammar Shall I Teach?" *English Journal* 47 (1958): 327-333.

Pooley, R. C. "Where Are We At?" *English Journal* 39 (1950): 496-504.

Postman, Neil. "Grammar and the Education Controversy." *English Journal* 49 (1960): 487-489.

Read, Charles. *Children's Categorization of Speech Sounds in English.* NCTE Research Report No. 17. Urbana, Ill.: National Council of Teachers of English, 1975.

Sager, Carol. "Improving the Quality of Written Composition in the Middle Grades." *Language Arts* 54 (1977): 760-762.

Sawkins, Margaret W. "What Children Say About Their Writing." In *The Writing Processes of Students.* Patrick J. Finn and Walter T. Petty, eds. Buffalo, N.Y.: State University of New York, 1975.

Scott, Fred Newton and Denny, Joseph Villiers. *Elementary English Composition.* Boston: Allyn and Bacon, 1900.

Sherman, Barry. "Reading for Meaning: Don't Let Word Study Blind Your Students." *Learning* 8 (1979): 40-44.

Smith, Dora V. Forward to *Children Learn to Write.* By Farinie J. Rogland. Chicago: National Council of Teachers of English, 1944.

Smith, Dora V. "The English Curriculum in Perspective—The Elementary School." *Elementary English Review* 23 (1946): 45-54.

Smith, Dora V. "English Language Arts: A Link Between Yesterday and Tomorrow." *English Journal* 42 (1953): 72-79.

Sommers, Nancy I. "Revision Strategies of Student Writers and Experienced Writers." Promising Research Award Speech. National Council of Teachers of English Convention, San Francisco, Calif.: November, 1979.

Sowers, Susan. "KDS CN RIT SUNR THN WE THINGK." *Learning: The Magazine for Creative Thinking,* in press.

Sowers, Susan. "A Six-Year-Old's Writing Process: The First Half of First Grade." *Language Arts* 56 (1979): 829-835.

Sowers, Susan. "Young Writers' Preference for Non-Narrative Modes of Composition." Paper presented at the Fourth Annual Boston University Conference on Language Development: September, 1979.

Squire, James R. "Composing—A New Emphasis for the Schools." In *The Writing Processes of Students.* Patrick J. Finn and Walter T. Petty, eds. Buffalo, N.Y.: State University of New York, 1975.

Stewig, John Warren. *Read and Write: Using Children's Literature as a Springboard to Writing.* New York: Hawthorn Books, Inc., 1975.

Strickland, Ruth G. *The Language Arts in the Elementary School.* 3rd ed. Lexington, Mass.: D. C. Heath & Co., 1969.

Strickland, Ruth G. "Some Basic Issues in the Teaching of English." *Phi Delta Kappan* 41 (1960): 332–335.

Thorndike, Edward L. "Scale for Measuring the Merit of English Writing." *Science* 33 (1911): 935–938.

Trabue, M. R. "Supplementing the Hillegas Scale." *Teachers College Record of Columbia University.* January 1917.

Tway, Eileen. "Why Not Try a Writer's Corner?" *On Righting Writing.* Ouida H. Clapp, ed. Urbana, Ill.: National Council of Teachers of English, 1975.

Witty, Paul A. and Martin, William. "An Analysis of Children's Compositions Written in Response to a Film." *Elementary English* 34 (1957): 158–163.

Witty, Paul. "Creative Writing Climates." *Childhood Education* 17 (1941): 253–257.

Yatvin, Joanne. "A Meaning-Centered Writing Program." *Phi Delta Kappan* 60 (1979): 680–681.

Contributors

Marlene Caroselli received her doctorate from the University of Rochester, studying the effect of parental involvement on students' writing. She has published several articles on this subject as well as conducting workshops on the local, state, and national levels. Currently, she is working for the Rochester City School District, Rochester, New York.

Patrick J. Finn is Associate Professor of Education at the State University of New York at Buffalo. He is author of numerous articles and editor of several publications on research in reading and writing.

Donald H. Graves is Professor of Education at the University of New Hampshire. He is currently Research Editor of *Language Arts*, Director of the Writing Process Laboratory, and has just completed a two-year study of the composing process of primary school children.

Shirley M. Haley-James is Associate Professor of Language Arts and Reading at Georgia State University in Atlanta. She is chair of the NCTE Committee on Teaching Written Composition in Grades 1 – 8 and serves as a member of the Steering Committee of the Elementary Section. Her publications include numerous journal articles and the co-authorship of *The Learning Center Idea Book*.

Roger A. McCaig is Director of Research and Development for the Grosse Pointe Public School System, Grosse Pointe, Michigan. In addition to various administrative positions in curriculum and instruction, he has fifteen years of experience as an English teacher. He has authored several articles and is a frequent lecturer and workshop leader.

Vera E. Milz is a primary level teacher at George P. Way Elementary School in Bloomfield Hills, Michigan. She has spoken on the development of writing in young children at a number of professional meetings and in-service programs across the country.

Walter T. Petty is Professor of Elementary and Remedial Education at the State University of New York at Buffalo. His publications include several journal articles on the teaching of writing as well as *Developing Children's Language* and *Experiences in Language*.

Joanne Yatvin is currently principal of Crestwood School in Madison, Wisconsin. She has taught at the elementary, middle, and high school levels as well as teaching remedial reading and English as a second language. She has published numerous articles in professional journals such as *English Journal, Phi Delta Kappan*, and *Learning*.